Parish Leadership Today

A Compilation of Writings
from Today's Parish

Twenty-Third Publications
P.O. Box 180
West Mystic, CT 06388

Second printing, 1980

Articles chosen and compiled by William V. Coleman

Cover , design and layout by Ed Curley
Library of Congress Catalog Card Number 79-65036
ISBN 0-89622-115-6

Contents

Contents

Preface

Pope John XXIII dreamed of a wide-reaching inner renewal of the Roman Catholic Church. Vatican II set the agenda for that renewal. After Vatican II, scores of theologians and pastoral theorists working in unison and separately provided the tools. Exciting new Church movements in religious education, liturgy, spirituality and collegial governance rushed into the consciousness of the Catholic who was used to a never-changing Church.

As we mark a decade and a half of efforts by the Church to renew and revitalize its life, we must ask the fundamental question, "Is progress being achieved?" In answer to this question we must focus attention not on movements or theories but on the local parish church: it is here that the vast majority of Catholics renew themselves or fail in the attempt.

So fundamental is the parish to the on-going life of the Church that we can say with confidence that any renewal which reaches that level is destined for success. Any renewal effort which leaves parishes untouched is doomed to ultimate failure.

Are parishes changing? Are they feeling the impact of renewal? To this question we must answer a resounding "yes." The changes are deeper than new liturgical forms, more appealing than bright new religion texts, more lasting than priests dressed in civilian clothing and called by their first names. The renewal of which we speak in this anthology is a renewal of the notion and practice of ministry itself.

To document this profound change in parish life we have chosen 13 essays from issues of the magazine, *Today's Parish*. Some of the essays are quite theoretical, others down-to-

5

earth and easily replicated in any parish setting. Some of the
essays are written by priests, some by laymen, and some by
women. All are involved in the renewal of American parish
life.

Section I of this anthology is entitled "The Church and Its
Leaders." Here you will encounter provocative thought on
the nature of a parish, the reason for leadership and the place
of the parish council in a changing theology of Church.

Section II contains three essays on the changing role of
leadership within the parish. Here are ideas about the clergy-
laity relationship, a view of the pastor as a talent scout and
some very perceptive thoughts on delegation of authority in a
parish setting. We call this section "New Approaches to
Leadership."

The parish council is a key element in parish renewal. Section III, "The Parish Council" attempts to define the work
of the council, the process of consensus decision making and
to offer a reason why councils often fail.

In our final section, "The Problems of Renewal," we look
at problems spawned by the success of parish renewal itself.
Among those problems are: the place of women in parish life,
the inhibitions rectories place on ministry, new ways to share
needed talent among parishes and the conditions necessary
for those who work for the Church.

All in all, our anthology breathes optimism about American parish life. So, too, do the pages of *Today's Parish*. In
those pages, each month, one discovers that both theorists
and practitioners of parish ministry are excited about the possibilities of renewal and are making giant steps in accomplishing what Pope John XXIII prayed for, the renewal of Catholic life.

Part I

The Parish and Its Leaders

The parish today is not what it used to be. All phases of Church life, from liturgy to ministry to management, differ from the parish past. Some parishioners are happy with most of the changes. Others find their relationship with the Church itself strained by these ongoing changes in parish life.

In this section, three well-known observers of the Church scene in America present penetrating analyses of the reasons for today's changing parish.

The section opens with a sociological-psychological look at what the parish is perceived to be by people who live there. This article was written by William V. Coleman, popular speaker, author and editor of the Parish Staff Section of *Today's Parish Magazine.*

The second article attempts to interpret leadership as a form of ministry to the Church. Too often, parish leaders feel guilty over the power they exercise. Power, however, is a legitimate tool to be used in the evangelization of others. Thomas Emmett, management specialist and parish consultant, concisely sets leadership in the broader perspective of ministry to others.

This section closes with a look at the parish council movement and its relationship to a changing theology of Church. This theological perspective is presented by Richard McBrien, professor at Boston College and well-known columnist, speaker and writer in the field of ecclesiology.

William V. Coleman

What Is A Parish?

The most rational way to evaluate anything is (1) to identify the ideal, (2) establish tolerance limits for deviation from the ideal and (3) measure what you are evaluating against those limits. Thus, if you are evaluating the condition of an automobile you look at the specifications, decide how closely the automobile comes to meeting the specifications, and then pass judgment on the car in question and its value to you.

Persons called upon to evaluate a parish quite reasonably seek to understand the ideal parish so that they can measure their parish against that ideal. The request for some perfect picture of parish is both reasonable and impossible to obtain.

The reason that the ideal picture of the parish is unattainable is that the parish is rooted not in changeless theology or revelation, but in Church law. The parish as we in America know it is more a product of the Council of Trent and the Second Council of Baltimore than the New Testament. To say this is not to say that the parish is outmoded or unnecessary, but simply to say that a clear definition which transcends legal categories is difficult to obtain. At best it is possible to give a series of definitions, each with some validity for some parishes. There can be no absolutes.

The word "parish" has Old Testament roots. It meant the believers at home with one another in a strange and alien land. For some in today's Church this expresses what the parish should be: a community of believers at home with one another in the midst of an unbelieving land.

This concept of parish supposes that each of the parishioners has personally appropriated faith in Jesus. It thinks of each parishioner as a believer who has undergone a deeply personal experience. The parish, then, is the support or reference group which helps the individual recall, keep alive and grow from that deep personal experience.

The liturgy in such a parish definition is a celebration of the personal faith. Whether it is initiation into faith at Baptism or return at Penance or memorial at Eucharist, all liturgy is reenactment of one's personal experience of Jesus through conversion.

The teaching necessary to sustain such a faith community is highly devotional. It seeks more than knowledge about religion and attempts to influence the day-to-day faith lives of parishioners. The qualities demanded of parish leaders are zeal in faith, sensitivity to conversion and personal holiness.

Few American parishes come close to this ideal. Charismatic prayer communities, at least during their early years, are more like this model than the territorial parish which must by law claim all who have been baptized and who live within the confines of the legally established limits.

Another concept of parish, similar but not identical to the community of faith idea, is the parish as a center to promote and preserve a particular style of life with roots in the past. It is ethnic not in the sense of common physical parentage, but in the sense of a common cultural tradition, a way of organizing life, a pattern of expected activity and the proclamation of certain values which underlie the patterns of action.

This concept of parish does not require personal faith in parishioners, only loyalty to the tradition and certain conformity to approved behavioral patterns. Those who behave properly are members in good standing.

The liturgy in such a model of parish is not so much a celebration of the death-resurrection of Jesus as it is a proclamation that one way of life is superior to all others. The teaching is highly moralistic in tone. The leadership is judged not on its personal holiness but on its loyalty to the tradition and its behavioral acceptance of the accepted style of life.

Both Protestant and Catholic parishes are often highly influenced by this model of parish. Their membership is united by the ideal way of life, their leadership measured by adherence to the lifestyle and their teaching highly moralistic. Personal faith is not a requisite for membership.

A third idea of parish is the more primitive one of the parish as the sacred ground. In this way of thinking, the parish is a place set apart from the sinful world. To it come the parishioners—soiled and stained from contact with the world—for rest and purification. It is an oasis in the desert of sinfulness.

Members of the parish are those who do not conform to the ways of the sinful world but who seek a higher life, usually one which is as unworldly as possible. No one is excluded from membership in the parish nor is membership really important. The parish is not so much people as a place where the individual meets with God.

Liturgy in such a concept is as unworldly as possible. Everything which marks it as different from day-to-day life is considered good, that which is like the sinful world unsuitable. Preaching is not important in this concept of parish; ceremony is.

The leaders of such a parish are judged competent if they are separated from the world. They must be like God, set apart, remote, aloof. As long as their personal lives do not give evidence of worldliness—temper, anger, sexuality, ambition—they are suitable ministers. Because these demands are unreal, leaders are seldom encountered in real life settings and seldom known as persons.

The monastic Church is the model of such a parish. Those who expect their parish to be like this are attracted to churches attached to monasteries or other enclosed religious communities. The typical American parish with its programs, its schools and its building drives is much too worldly to measure up to this ideal.

A fourth model of the parish is that of political party. In this model the parish is a group of people embued with a program for social reform, based on the teachings of Jesus. The true members are those who subscribe to the program and who work for it either directly or indirectly by their contributions and support.

Liturgy in such a parish model provides the inspiration to continue the work of reform. Its ceremonies are less important than its preaching. The preaching is centered in applying the words of the Gospel to the social problems of the here and now world. The leadership is considered competent not by its personal holiness but by its knowledge of the program and its ability to apply this knowledge to the social problems of the local or national community.

Some few American parishes come close to this ideal or at least they did during the late 1960s and early 1970s. Usually, however, these were parishes composed of upper middle class, highly educated people who were searching for some new understanding of religion. Poorer people and the less educated have rarely felt comfortable with such a parish vision.

A final understanding of the parish is that it is an extension of the school, an institution which presents programs to upgrade the quality of its members' lives. These programs extend from the cradle to the grave. They include programs for children, youth and adults of all ages.

Like any school, the real vitality resides not with the pupils but with the staff. The liturgy is educational. It is planned by the staff for the people, to help them become more alert or more aware of the truth the staff already knows. The teaching is determined by the staff with some reference to the needs of the people as viewed by the staff.

The leadership of the parish is the parish staff, supplemented by the few loyal laypeople who help them with their duties. Leadership is established by professional training rather than by faith, zeal or other personal qualities, no matter how inspired.

Many American parishes approach this ideal, either because the staff intends this ideal or because they are unable to stimulate greater participation by the people they are sent to serve.

All of these ideals are a part of the historical tradition of parish. All of them reflect the thinking of some of the parishioners in the average parish. As a parish evaluation team approaches the tricky task of helping the parish to improve its offerings, and to grow into a more fully-developed church structure, these models will often surface in conversation. They will underlie many of the assumptions made by committee members.

What is important to realize is that none of these ideals is absolute. None of them offers a complete picture of the parish. Each is suitable for some sets of circumstances and unsuitable for others. Tolerance of differing views will go a long way in helping any committee reach consensus.

Thomas Emmett

Leadership Is Ministry

Across the country one experiences a pressing need to share leadership functions within a parish setting. Individual parishes, or more accurately the priests in these parishes, are more and more being confronted with an overwhelming number of tasks. Parishes are finally realizing that no one person has either the time or the skills to accomplish all that must be done. Leadership and service must be shared—the concept of ministry broadened.

A response to this need for broadening has emerged under the heading of "team ministry" or "shared responsibility." Shared ministry has passed through several stages. Seven years ago, team ministry designated a group of priests who worked together in a parish setting without a designated pastor. Then, team or shared ministry referred to salaried professionals—priests, Sisters, and lay people—who formed a nucleus at the center of the parish. It was intended that this professional staff would use their leadership role and skills in activating and developing the initiative of the whole parish community.

Now, and in the future, team ministry, or shared responsibility, is being extended even further to include nonprofessional parishioners in leadership roles: parish coordinators of religious education, parish workers, and members of various boards and councils.

As with most change, this sharing of ministry has evoked both excitement and disappointment. For the excitement of participating as leaders in a parish decision-making process not to lead to disappointment, an understanding of the broadened concept of ministry is essential.

This broadening must take place not only on the intellectual level, but also on the practical level. A real concept of ministry must be translated into one's life style. This will re-

quire modification of personal habits and behavior in the life
of some current Church leaders.

Before defining roles, analyzing styles of leadership, sharing responsibility, and working as a team, we must ground
the whole endeavor on a renewed base. We must have solid
theological understanding of ministry and the ministerial
framework of the Church. Once this grounding takes place, a
major obstacle to collegiality in practical parish terms will be
overcome.

We begin our examination of ministry with the command
of Jesus—"Love one another as I have loved you." This imperative to all his followers was clearly exemplified in Jesus'
life. Often we associate Jesus' love for mankind too narrowly
with his passion and his death. Jesus showed his love for us,
not only by suffering and dying, but also by showing us the
way, the truth, and the light throughout his whole life.

Jesus' life of personal loving service (ministry) climaxed
and was summarized by the ultimate act of self-giving for
others—his passion and death. Jesus' life of personal loving
service and self-oblation to the Father is what constituted Jesus as priest and minister.

All those who have entered the Christian community and
profess to be Christians are obliged to continue the redemptive work of Jesus. They must lead lives modelled on his life
of love and service. Participation in Jesus' priesthood, in a
broad sense, is required of all Christians regardless of whether or not they are now community leaders.

St. Paul recognized that the whole Church shares and continues the personal loving service of Jesus, but various members do this in different ways. There are many gifts or charisms within the Christian community. All of them are given
by the Holy Spirit for the service of the whole body.

For the Christian community to exemplify in its own life
the personal loving service commanded by Jesus, certain individuals are called upon by the community to enable it to ful-
fill its mission of service to the world.

We can view the ministry of those individuals called or designated by the community as an enabling ministry, ministry
in the narrow sense, in relation to the *primary* ministry of service in the broader sense.

Necessary Ingredients

It should be noted that to be an enabling minister and to exercise leadership, three very necessary ingredients must be present. First, the individual must be gifted (charismed) and called by the Spirit. He or she must have a vocation.

Second, the community must recognize the individual's charism, or discern the presence of the Spirit.

Third, the community must designate the individual to use his or her gift in the service and development of the whole Christian community.

Looking, then, upon the Church as charismatically structured, we can describe her as a fellowship of the gifts of the Spirit, a fellowship of different ministries. Each individual's charism contributes to the development of the whole community and is necessary for the community to be able ("enabled") to carry out its primary ministry of loving service.

All charisms are given by the same Spirit and are, in fact, manifestations of that Spirit operative in the community. For this reason, conflict among the ministers, maneuvering for positions of prestige, and plays for power should have no place.

One practical way to eliminate these all-too-common maladies that affect shared ministry would be to have centers where all having charisms needed by and for the community could be trained and their skills developed. While gaining a greater appreciation of one's unique contribution to building the whole community, a more realistic approach to team ministry and shared responsibility would be attained.

This approach to ministry does invert the traditional pyramidal approach. Instead of ministry being defined from the top down, . . . "It is defined," in the words of Rosemary Reuther, "from its foundation in the people and seen as arising out of the people . . . The people do not lose their power by designating certain persons to exercise it. They merely articulate their own functions thereby . . . The leadership use their role and skills to motivate and develop the initiative of the whole community, rather than to pacify it in relation to themselves."

In attempting to exercise leadership, bring about renewal and function as a change agent, the minister-leader must "deal with people." At the same time he must accomplish specific tasks. How well the minister-leader balances the tension between person and task will determine how effectively he will be able to share ministry and responsibility on the parish team. It would be helpful at this point to discuss alternative styles of leadership in general.

Styles of Leadership

Five definite approaches to leadership are briefly described below:

1. *Impoverished leader.* In his approach, this leader, or non-leader, emphasizes neither people nor task, and avoids involvement. This person's style of leadership can be characterized as "iffy." Since he feels he cannot really change another person, he sees his task as merely telling people the expectations, getting out of their way, and letting them decide what to do.

2. *Task Leader or Autocrat.* Being chiefly concerned with the task and viewing people only in relation to their contribution to the task, the task leader plans, directs, and controls the behavior of those he is trying to change or lead. The task leader uses power and coercion to train others in the "right" way (his way) to do things.

3. *Counsellor leader or "Active Listener."* With primary emphasis on people and minimal emphasis on task, this leader's main concern is with interpersonal relationships. The task of this leader is one of support and encouragement to the other person without the judgmental pressure of others' values, including the leader's, being introduced.

4. *Middle-of-the-road leader.* A person using this style of leadership emphasizes finding satisfactory and workable solutions through balancing and compromising procedures. Since he feels that people accept suggestions from people they respect, he sees one of his tasks as gaining enough prestige and respect to influence others. This approach is regularly employed by any good salesman in winning others over to his

product. In time the customer will learn that his brand is better than Brand X.

5. *Team leader.* With emphasis on the interdependence of people, this leader has maximal concern for task and people. The task of the team leader is one of creating conditions under which people can consider present behavior and weigh possible alternatives. They learn to change, and ultimately change themselves.

Team Leader: First Choice

All minister-leaders walk a tight rope between accomplishing their broad task of building community and working effectively for the individual persons within that community. These leaders manifest all the styles of leadership from "iffy" to "team." However, the one style most preferred and used most often by those engaged in sharing ministry is that of the team leader.

This style of leadership ties in closely with our understanding of the minister as an enabler, facilitator, and growth producer. Using this approach, the team leader gives the necessary guidance and direction for the accomplishing of a task. At the same time, the team leader allows the person being led the opportunity to consider his present position, to experiment with various alternatives, and buy into the leader's.

The team leader is a risk-taker, a person of faith. The one being led may not buy the leader's position. On the other hand, the team leader has still been effective, for the other is growing, developing, learning.

I have tried to sketch out a theology of ministry which provides a basis for all leadership within the Church. I have described very briefly the diverse styles of and approaches to leadership. I have singled out team leader as the one preferred in this age of "shared ministry."

The next step, logically, would be for the minister-leaders to engage as a team, in systematic leadership and team-building training. A gap exists between appreciating leadership as ministry, intellectually, in the isolation of a lonely office and facing the very real demands of leadership and ministry in relation to the other members of the team.

The resolution of these issues is fundamental to the success
of leadership and ministry.

Richard McBrien

The Place of Parish Councils Within the Developing Theology of the Church

The term "Catholic Action" was a prominent part of our Roman Catholic vocabulary in the 1940s and even into the 1950s. If there is anyone who can recall the term and, better still, who can precisely define it, then you must appreciate more than most how far we Catholics have come in our understanding of the place of the laity in the Church.

Less than 15 or 20 years ago you would have been regarded as an entirely progressive and forward-looking Catholic if you looked upon the lay apostolate as "a participation in the apostolate of the hierarchy." This, by the way, is the exact definition of *Catholic Action.*

Today, under the impact of a burst of theological reflection and of the Second Vatican Council itself, Catholics have come to see that the concept of Catholic Action offered too narrow a base for the lay apostolate within the Church.

"The lay apostolate," the Council's Dogmatic Constitution on the Church declares, "is a participation in the saving mission of the Church itself. Through their baptism and confirmation, all are commissioned to that apostolate by the Lord Himself" (n. 33). Indeed the same conciliar document had earlier insisted that the mission of the Church, the People of God, "applies equally to the laity, religious, and clergy" (n. 30).

In the years before the Council, most Catholics, and certainly those of us who were studying for the priesthood or already functioning as priests, understood the Church in primarily hierarchical terms. We perceived the Church first and

19

foremost as an institution, a hierarchically structured means of salvation founded by Christ. The mission of the Church was twofold: to teach saving truth and to make available saving grace. A duly constituted and validly ordained priesthood was absolutely essential if this dual purpose was to be served. Only those officially designated could preach and teach the content of Christian faith, and only those sacramentally set apart had the power to make present and administer the mysteries of this faith.

I am not suggesting, of course, that things have changed now to the point where the Church is no longer concerned about salvation, that her mission no longer includes preaching the Word and celebrating the sacraments, or that ordained priesthood is of no importance to her life and work. What I am stressing is, in most cases, a matter of degree and emphasis.

Clearly, the emphasis in the pre-Vatican II Catholic Church was on the ordained rather than the non-ordained, on ecclesiastical authority and unilateral decision-making rather than on lay initiative and shared responsibility. Many otherwise sophisticated textbooks taught that Christ founded the Church as a monarchical institution. All power was given in the first instance to Peter and to his successors, the Popes. They, in turn, could share that power with bishops who, in turn, could delegate their share of papal power to their priests. It was almost as if Christ established the Church as one parish with one pastor, the Pope. That we have many dioceses and parishes today came about only because the Pope inevitably found it impossible to administer the whole Church by himself.

At the risk of oversimplifying—and some oversimplification may be unavoidable—I should suggest again that the usual preconciliar view of the Church, commonly accepted by Catholics before 1962, regarded the Church primarily as a visible society. It was hierarchically structured, whose mission was the salvation of souls accomplished through the preaching of the Word and the administration of the sacraments.

This particular theory of the Church, in turn, provided the

basis for a whole complexus of attitudes, values, and customs adopted by Catholics in these preconciliar years. Thus, we had a generally clericalized liturgy (no dialogue Mass, no communal responses of any sort, except for the prayers after Mass; no lay participation in the sacred action itself, except for the role of the altar boys). Pastoral authority was exercised according to a monarchical pattern (no parish or diocesan pastoral councils, no priests' senates, no instruments of pastoral accountability, no limitation on term of office). And laity were included in the work of the Church only under very limited and carefully circumscribed conditions (e.g., as in "Catholic Action").

We should not exaggerate the role and impact of the Second Vatican Council. It did not *initiate* the process of change. It was, more exactly, an important part of the process itself. On the other hand, Vatican II was indeed a major force in the alteration of Catholic consciousness on key questions of Catholic faith and order.

It was, for example, the Council's teaching on collegiality that tended to set aside the usual assumptions about the Church-as-monarchy. The Pope is not portrayed in the Council documents as an absolute monarch. On the contrary, the Council teaches specifically that bishops are not merely vicars, or stand-ins, for the Pope (Lumen Gentium, n. 27). "Together with its head, the Roman Pontiff, and never without this head, the episcopal order is the subject of supreme and full power over the universal Church" (L.G., n. 22). In addition, "the supreme authority with which this college is empowered over the whole Church is exercised in a solemn way through an ecumenical council."

But collegiality means more than the sharing of ecclesiastical power and responsibility among the Pope and the other bishops. It applies also, and one might even say "especially," to the relationships that must exist among all the local churches—all the dioceses and parishes and special communities—which constitute the Church universal. In the words of the Council's Dogmatic Constitution on the Church: "This collegial union is apparent also in the mutual relations of the individual bishops with particular churches and with the universal Church. . . . This variety of local churches with one common aspiration is particularly splendid evidence of the catholicity of the undivided Church" (L.G., n. 23).

What is being asserted here, and elsewhere in the council documents, is the exceedingly important doctrine of the "local church"—a doctrine too often underemphasized in the years before the council. The Church is not, in fact, one large parish subdivided into dioceses and smaller parishes for the sake of administrative efficiency. The Church is rather a community of local churches, the totality of which constitutes the Church universal. In a very real sense, the Church, the Body of Christ, is present wherever there is a community of men and women who acknowledge the Lordship of Jesus; who gather from time to time for the breaking of the bread and the sharing of the cup; who are summoned by the proclamation of God's holy Word; who are bound together in the fellowship of the Holy Spirit; who accept a common responsibility for the application of the Gospel of Jesus Christ to their own lives, to the lives of those outside their community and to the whole of mankind.

Impact on Parish Councils

What does all this have to do with parish councils? Vatican II's teaching on the local church reminds us of the exalted status that each parish does in fact have within the universal Church. Those who participate in the life of a particular church are participating in the life of the Body of Christ itself, in that particular place. The Lord and his Risen Spirit are present in that particular place, within that particular community. The quality of their lives, the quality of their response to the redemptive presence of Christ and his Spirit, will determine, for good or for ill, the quality of the Church's mission—and also define the effectiveness of her specific role as the sign of Christ in that place, at that time, under those circumstances.

Each church, in union with one another and in union with the Pope—who stands in their midst as a symbol of their unity with one another—is the Body of Christ in its own place, through its own people.

Those people, in turn, are held responsible by baptism for the quality of Christian life and mission in that place, in that local church. Just as the Church universal is not constituted by the Pope alone, as if he were its absolute monarch, but by the Pope and the bishops together. So, too, the local church is not constituted or formed by the bishop alone but by the bishop and all of the Catholic people in that place: laity, as well as clergy.

"As sharers in the role of Christ the Priest, the Prophet, and the King," the Council declared, "the laity have an active part to play in the life and activity of the Church" (Decree on the Apostolate of the Laity, n. 10).

Indeed, "everything which the Dogmatic Constitution on the Church has said so far in its second chapter on 'The People of God' applies equally to the laity, religious, and clergy" (L.G. 30). The "lay apostolate" is indeed a sharing in "the saving mission of the Church itself" (n. 33).

Furthermore, the Council insisted, pastors themselves must realize that the mission of the Church was not given to them alone. Rather it is "the noble duty" of pastors "so to shepherd the faithful and recognize their services and charismatic gifts that all according to their proper roles may cooperate in this common undertaking with one heart" (L.G. 30).

Such pastors must "recognize and promote the dignity as well as the responsibility of the layman in the Church." Pastors must "willingly make use of his prudent advice." They must "confidently assign duties to (the laity) in the service of the Church, allowing (the laity) freedom and room for action." The layperson is to be encouraged "so that he may undertake tasks on his own initiative" (L.G. 37).

But the Council, of course, went beyond general abstract statements. It mandated an institutional and structural application of these lofty theological principles. In the words of the Decree on the Apostolate of the Laity: "In dioceses, as far as possible, there should be *councils which assist the apostolic work of the Church;* note the text did not say 'assist the apostolic work of the bishop' either in the field of making the Gospel known and men holy, or in the charitable, social, and other spheres. To this end, *clergy and religious should appropriately cooperate with the laity.* Again, note that the text does not say: 'clergy and religious should enlist the aid of the laity' " (n. 26).

Elsewhere the Council declares, "It is highly desirable that in each diocese a pastoral council be established over which the diocesan bishop himself will preside and in which specially chosen clergy, religious, and lay people will participate" (Decree on the Bishop's Pastoral Office in the Church, n. 27).

Nowhere, of course, is the Council's broadened understanding of the Church as the total community of laity, religious, and clergy more strikingly apparent than in its calling the Church "the People of God." Its wide-ranging concern for liturgical renewal and reform serves to bring out more forcefully the truth that it is the whole community, not just the celebrating priest, which is directly and intimately involved in this supreme act of worship.

In a sense, it follows that the community that worships together as a community must be prepared to deliberate together as a community. It must decide as far as possible, what the needs and tasks of its local church are, and how they are best fulfilled. This is why a parish council—and, at a higher level, a diocesan pastoral council—exists. It is the representative organ of the whole local church.

Through the council, the entire local church accepts the responsibility that is its own through baptism, a responsibility for the total mission of the Church. That mission is to proclaim its faith in the Lordship of Jesus both in word and in sacrament, to offer itself as a sign or sacrament of the risen Lord's presence among us, and to employ its resources generously in the service of those in need. Also the pursuit of justice is itself a "constitutive dimension of the preaching of the Gospel," as the synodal document "Justice in the World" declares.

Shared Responsibility

Since the adjournment of the Second Vatican Council in December, 1965, there has been some confusion about the meaning of collegiality and shared responsibility within the Church. On the one hand, some Catholics, generally uneasy about change and reform, have argued that collegiality was meant to apply only to the relationship between the Pope and the bishops. Shared responsiblity may be good, but it affects only the hierarchy.

Others, meanwhile, have suggested that collegiality must apply beyond the papal-episcopal relationship, but they, too, tend to confine its meaning and scope. This second group, usually priests, suggests that collegiality applies only to the papal-episcopal relationship, on the one hand, and the epis-copal-presbyterial relationship, on the other, i.e., collegiality also requires that bishops share their power and authority with their priests, specifically through a priests' senate.

Neither of these two views is correct. First, it is clear from recent Catholic theology—and it is at least implied in the Council Documents themselves—that collegiality covers more than the relationship between Pope and bishops. Second, the view that collegiality must not go beyond the rela-tionship between a bishop and his priests is itself a new kind of clericalism. This time, however, it operates under the guise of liberal or progressive thought. If one priest—pope, bishop, pastor—makes all the decisions, we call that a cleri-calization of ecclesiastical authority. But if 25 priests make all the decisions affecting the whole diocese, why is that any less a clericalization of authority? We have simply multiplied the clerical factor by 25.

No, the Council's and contemporary Catholic theology's teaching on the meaning and scope of collegiality are broader than these post-conciliar views. Collegiality means that the Church is itself a community of local churches, all of which together constitute the Church universal. The bishop of each local church, or diocese, functions as a symbol of unity for that local church, and his union with all the other bishops is, in turn, a symbol of union existing among all other local churches. The Pope serves, finally, as a symbol of unity with-in the college of bishops. The Petrine ministry, as even the 1974 Catholic-Lutheran consensus statement acknowledged, is a necessary ministry serving the entire body of the entire local community in a given cluster of local churches, which we call a diocese.

The laity do, and must, participate in these representative bodies known as councils because the laity, as well as the clergy and religious, are responsible for the mission of the Church. Such responsibility is initially given in Baptism, then sealed in Confirmation, and signified again and again in the Eucharist. It is a responsibility given not by the bishop or by the pastor but, as Vatican II declares, "by the Lord Himself" (L.G. 33).

We, of course, keep coming back to the theology, which I have attempted to outline, and which I have expressed much more fully in my book, *The Remaking of the Church: An Agenda for Reform.* Roman Catholics, and Roman Catholic clergy included, oppose the creation and existence of effective parish councils because they are convinced that Christ established his Church as a monarchy. The Pope is its one absolute monarch; bishops share in the papal monarchical power at the diocesan level; and pastors are intended by Christ to share in that same monarchical power and authority at the parish level.

This theology does not coincide with the official teaching of the Second Vatican Council. The Church is not a monarchy; it is collegial in structure. The Church is a communion of local churches. Each baptized Christian participates in the saving mission of the Church itself. The Christian's participation in the mission of the Church derives not from the mandate of the bishop or the pastor but from the mandate of the Lord Himself. This mandate is communicated through the sacraments of Baptism and Confirmation, and ratified again and again in the Eucharist. The Church is the whole community of those who are called to acknowledge the Lordship of Jesus. The responsibility for the Church's mission belongs in principle to all. Parish councils are one important way in which that theological principle can be implemented and realized.

Where Are We Going?

This concept will be of no interest either to pessimists or utopians. The pessimists believe that nothing good can or will happen in the Church. Parish councils are a good and worthy idea, they say, but it's an idea that either can't work, or won't be allowed to work. The utopians, on the other hand, are content to say that everything is going to work out just fine—with or without our expenditure of energy. If parish councils are good for the Church, then, of course, the Church will accept them and they will prosper *per omnia saecula saeculorum.*

The pessimists, in my view, are contradicted by the evidence of progress already achieved, the weaknesses and deficiencies of the parish council movement notwithstanding. The utopians, it seems to me, are contradicted by the constant Catholic tradition that grace builds on nature, that God's gifts require our receptivity and cooperation if they are to take effect. Roman Catholicism has rejected Quietism just as vigorously as it has rejected Pelagianism. Salvation is not so totally the work of God that it requires no human effort, nor is it so totally the work of man that it depends utterly and completely on the quality of the individual's effort.

Between pessimism and utopianism there lies the position that one might call simply "Christian realism." The Kingdom can be ours, but not automatically, nor merely by reason of our own efforts.

For the Christian realist, the parish council movement in the United States can have a successful and fruitful future if the Church in America takes seriously the following agenda for institutional purification and growth:

1. The diocesan leadership, and the bishop in particular, must be personally committed to the conciliar principle. If parish councils are mandated simply because it is a requirement of Vatican II, and not at all because the leadership sees the intrinsic value of parish councils, then the conciliar process will not genuinely take root in a diocese.

2. Parish councils in the future must be more sensitive to the implications of their present membership composition. Greater efforts will have to be made to include women, young people, blacks, and Spanish speaking in their deliberations.

3. Parish councils must broaden their ecclesiological vision. The mission of the Church is the coming of God's King-

dom. The Church is called to proclaim the Lordship of Jesus, to announce by word and by sacrament that God is reconciling the world to Himself through Jesus Christ and his risen Spirit. The Church is also called to offer itself as a sign of God's redemptive presence among us, which is but another way of speaking of the Kingdom. The quality of our lives, not only individually but corporately, will determine the credibility of our claim that God is indeed present amongst His people. And finally the Church is called to use its resources generously and imaginatively to heal the wounds which divide the human community, to reconcile what has been alienated, to renew what has decayed and become lifeless. As the document "Justice in the World" of the Third International Synod of Bishops (Rome, 1971) declares: "Action on behalf of justice and participation in the transformation of the world fully appear to us as a constitutive dimension of the preaching of the Gospel, or, in other words, of the Church's mission for the redemption of the human race and its liberation from every oppressive situation."

4. Parish councils to thrive must be more genuinely ecumenical in outlook and practice. We are not alone in the Body of Christ. There are other Christians whom the Second Vatican Council reminded us "have a right to be honored by the title of Christian" (Decree on Ecumenism, n. 3). The mission of the Church belongs to all Christians, not to Catholics alone. That is stated without prejudice to the Roman Catholic conviction that Roman Catholicism is, in principle, the fullest expression of the ecclesial reality.

5. There must be broader and more far-reaching institutional reforms of the Catholic Church if we are to change the present situation. Now, for all practical purposes, the quality of parish councils depends so fully on the quality of pastoral leadership and commitment. This raises many questions: the election of bishops, the accountability of pastors, the canonical authority of parish councils once constituted (are they merely consultative, or are they deliberative as well, i.e., genuine decision-making bodies?), the nature and orientation of seminary education and formation, and other related issues. Our assorted hopes for the success of parish councils cannot

be isolated from our hopes and concerns about the continued renewal and reform of the entire Body of Christ, in earthly head as well as in faithful members.

May the Spirit of the risen Christ strengthen us in our resolve and lead us to its fruition.

Part II

New Approaches to Leadership

One of the root differences between the parish of old and today's parish is the style of leadership exercised by the clergy and all others who share the leadership role. This change in leadership style is not limited to the Church. It is present in government, in corporate board rooms, in schools and in all our institutions.

In this section are three essays about the new style of leadership in the Church. The first is by the noted liturgist, William J. Freburger, now editor of *Celebration* homily service. He explains how ministry in the Church has widened to include people from all walks of life. George Martin, one of the founders of the Charismatic Movement within the Church addresses the new role of the pastor as the coordinator of charisms. The section closes with an article by adult educator Leon McKenzie on the art of delegation.

All seek to explore the possibilities and the pitfalls of the new style of leadership only now beginning to emerge in the American parish.

Part II

New Approaches to Leadership

William J. Freburger

Cracking the Ministry Myth

Let's hear it for the American Church! Let's hear it for us! No other national Church has as many persons and resources committed to ministry. No other national Church is offering as many opportunities for the Spirit to work in the midst of his people.

Explore further! No other national Church has our fund of experience; the Germans may ponder the theology of ministry, the French may generate brilliant illustrations of ministry, but only we can tell them what it's like. We've been there. We're doing it.

Perhaps this is an optimistic evaluation of the present state of ministry here in the United States. Okay, then, here's the bad news. We do find ourselves having to justify a diversity of ministerial roles in our communities.

The common justification is the lack of ordained ministers who in the past filled these roles. Or if numbers were available, they would be ready to assume the new tasks that now call for our attention. But this justification out of practical need often provokes frustration. Why do we have to wait for circumstances to force us into the creation of new ministries or into expanding present ministerial roles? Our ideals and our theology already demand this of us.

This dissonance may be the source of frustration, but it has also sparked an unparalleled pastoral creativity in the Catholic Church in this country. Our "theologizing" is not the sterile citation of proofs for or against a stated position; rather, we are engaged in the exciting task of interpreting our experience. We have discovered some embarrassing differences between what we desire and what we do. We are slowly—yes, slowly but surely—beginning to rearrange structures and rela-

33

tionships. At last we are beginning to incarnate values which are now missing or shadowed.

During the first 50 years of this century, our ecclesial life in the United States gave birth to a gift which we offered to the universal Church. That gift was accepted and enshrined in the Declaration on Religious Liberty of the Second Vatican Council. Now, in this last half of the 20th century, we are preparing a second gift for the whole Church. It is the gift of ministry.

Up until very recently, our understanding of ministry developed with almost exclusive concentration on one type of ministry, the ordained. Such ministry was absolute, with only tenuous reference to the community. But the liturgical reform of the past decade has given us a vocabulary with which to articulate our growing experience of ministry. It is not strange that a renewed liturgy would serve as a foundation for a renewal of ministries. It is when we worship, especially in the Eucharist, that we are most the Church. Because we manifest in worship the real nature of the true Church, the nature of our liturgy demands that a Church which worships with diverse ministries should also be living out of diverse ministries. It was the liturgy which first revealed the gap between our preaching and our practice.

As a result of our American experience we are launched upon a project which no other national Church is tackling. We are dealing with the role of women in ministry. The beginnings of the project have been met with obtuseness and fear; there has been much misunderstanding and not a little pettiness. But the atmosphere has already begun to change. We cannot go back, because we have already advanced! We know that our American experience rings true. It is a sad fact of cultural differences that our society may be the only one in which the questions about the role of women can be raised. We have begun to ask the questions and to examine our perceptions of reality. These initial steps alone have caused others—even some here at home—to characterize us as "outlandish." But we cannot deny the validity of what we have seen with our eyes and known with our hearts.

Ministry In Our Midst

I suggest a process for continuing this discernment about ministry in our midst. The procedure which I recommend is very simple and is couched in a series of questions. We can ask these questions of ourselves as individuals, but they should be shared and discussed in the communities of which we are a part. These questions are really an agenda for group discernment.

The first question is: Who are you? What this question should elicit is your appreciation of your ministry; continuing, what is the community you serve, how do you serve it, what areas do you consciously neglect or avoid, where are you ministering without awareness? Another question is implied in this first question: do you like what you are doing?

The second question is meant for the group: who are we right now? As with the first question, this second should open us to the following considerations: How is ministry taking place right now in our community? Who is doing ministry? What are they doing? To whom, when, how? How many of these ministers are perceived and accepted as such by the community? Who is ministering in our midst without a ministerial identification?

An example may help clarify the purposes of this second question. At the present time in our American parishes, there are persons who are ministers, but we do not call them that. Because we do not perceive them as ministers, we do not treat them or their ministry seriously. One of the most important ministers in any parish can be the rectory housekeeper or the parish secretary or both. These are the people with whom callers, on the phone or at the door, make first contact. The harassed housekeeper who is preparing supper and answering the phone is often driven to gruffness or curtness. Some parishes solve the dilemma by hiring local teenagers, at 50 cents an hour, to "rectory-sit." These circumstances go beyond questions about the public image that the parish is presenting. Even more important is the ministerial blindspot which is revealed by such practices. Hence, the second question.

All of these questions have a hidden hook which will become immediately apparent in a group's discerning. Each member of the group will have his or her own understanding and perception of ministry. There will be real differences on these matters within the group itself. We must articulate these differences in order to handle them properly.

For this reason, the second question about actual ministering leads to the third question: what is the understanding of ministry implied in the identification and evaluation which I have made in response to the second question? This third question does not call for the justification of a theological position. It merely requests exposition, not argument. Why do we see certain persons as ministers, and not others?

The fourth question is similar to the third; indeed, it is the third question applied to the community. Why are we doing what we are doing? What does our present use of ministers say about our appreciation of Church, of community, of mission? One of the results of this question may be the interesting discovery that we have no reason for some of the things that we do, except the universal justification "We've always done it this way." For instance, why is it always the youngest priest-associate who is given charge of youth activities in a parish? What is it about a newly ordained, pastorally inexperienced priest that fits such a person to be a moderator of youth, a very important ministry in today's Church? Is the answer as obvious as you think it is?

The fifth question moves us toward a summary; what do we like about this evaluation of ministry in our community? Where do we need to improve? How can we validate ministry in the perception of the community? How can we lovingly but firmly retire from ministry those incompetent or incapable of their roles? This fifth question will lead to tasks, for no community can be completely satisfied with its present structure of ministries. I make that assertion with absolute certainty, because as of this writing the Parousia has not yet occurred.

But don't go away yet: there is a sixth and final question. It is the question behind all the preceding questions; indeed, it is the most important question about ministry: how can we love one another more, so that we may serve others better?

It is a good question with which to end all meetings. Later, in the stillness of the night, some answers may occur!

George Martin

The Pastor As Talent Scout

"Priest crisis" is a strong, even frightening, phrase. And yet a bishop in the midwest has bleakly warned that a priest crisis lies ahead for his diocese. With the median age of his priests already at 45, and with few seminarians on the way to ordination, simple arithmetic convinces him that within five years his diocese will experience a real pinch.

It would be easy to feel fleeting compassion for this bishop and "his" problem and let it go at that. But, unfortunately, "his" problem is increasingly becoming "our" problem, no matter in which diocese we live. While national statistics are hard to come by, I have a very strong hunch that lean days lie ahead for most dioceses.

It is not that looming ahead is a sudden and dramatic drop in the number of priests available; it is rather that there will be a steadily advancing median age of active priests, a steady erosion of the number of priests available for pastoral ministry, and an increasing workload for those priests still manning the trenches.

How serious we consider the situation will depend upon our perspective. If we view the Church as a holding operation, if we are content to have the minimum weekly requirement of sacramental life made available, if we are looking only for sheer institutional survival, then the situation might not be considered alarming.

But if our hopes for the Church are higher, if we expect the Church to have a significant impact on the life of its members, if we want the Church to be present to the world in mission—then the steady dwindling of those we have always relied upon for leadership is disturbing. And if we feel the Church is now carrying out its mission with a less than desirable degree of effectiveness and vision, a crisis in the leadership ranks can only compound our concern.

The obvious reaction of most Catholics might be: "Well, the Church must simply learn to rely more and more on lay leadership." I agree: the Church must do just that.

Tapping Lay Leadership

But how is this going to happen? And how is it going to happen quickly enough and in sufficient measure to make a real difference as the time of vanishing clergy presses hard upon us?

Assuredly lay leadership exists in the Church right now. There are more than 2,000 permanent deacons already ordained (although they technically are not "lay"), and another 2,000 plus are in training. Parish councils are functioning in increasing numbers of parishes. There are extraordinary ministers of the Eucharist and directors of religious education as well as religious women serving as members of pastoral teams. Much progress has made the "pray, pay and obey" days a dim, unmissed memory.

But there is still a long, long way to go.

Ask yourself: how would your parish operate if no priest were permanently assigned to it? What would happen if a priest came from a neighboring parish only to say Mass on Sunday? What if there were no longer enough priests available for your parish to have a resident pastor? Sadly, some parishes are already experiencing this deprivation.

Many activities would probably go on as usual. The parish council would gulp a little, and then settle down to the task of keeping the electric bills paid and the roof repaired. It would be very desirable for them to do a lot more, but the "missions accomplished" of most parish councils too seldom exceed this level.

The board of education would continue to oversee the religious education programs, relying more and more on its full time coordinator for advice in setting major directions. Most parish societies would continue to function as usual. Parish activities would go on, unabated, though doubtless diminished.

In fact, things might appear as though they were going

well. Some parishioners might even wonder what it was that good old Father Smith did, before the bishop sent him away for an extended rest to recover from his chronic exhaustion.

But what of the spiritual mission of the parish? Would anyone be concerned about the growth of the parish into a Christian community? Would anyone guide the parish in taking initiative to accomplish the different aspects of its mission: evangelizing, meeting the needs of the poor, building ecumenical bridges with other congregations, revitalizing the faith of its lukewarm members?

Unless lay members of the parish had been involved in these aspects of parish life in the past, it is doubtful that they would be able to exert much leadership in these areas in the absence of a resident pastor. And I believe that at best the prevailing pattern today is for the laity to be passive participants in many essential dimensions of the parish's spiritual mission.

How can parishes more effectively involve members in different phases of mission? What should a pastor do to "get people involved"? How is lay leadership developed? These are current and demanding questions, even without the looming spectre of a "priest crisis."

The Catholic Church has traditionally relied upon what is basically a volunteer system to meet its various manpower needs. Priests are first of all volunteers: they stepped forward to go to the seminary. They were subjected to careful screening along the way—but the priesthood is made up of those who volunteered for service to the Church.

Our parishes are largely run on a volunteer basis. Those who offer themselves for service find that their generosity is almost invariably accepted. The people who make up, for example, the worship commission, are usually those who volunteered for the job.

This volunteer system has been slightly modified by the American penchant for democracy: the members of our councils and boards are elected to office. However, this is really only a modification of the volunteer system: men and women volunteer to run for office. Sometimes there are barely enough volunteers to fill out the ballot.

"So what's wrong with the volunteer system?" you might ask. "Is there any better alternative?"

The weakness of the volunteer system is that it is essentially a passive approach to meeting the Church's leadership needs. There is an analogy to a company that needs to hire highly skilled nuclear scientists, but instead of going out to recruit them, simply hopes that some qualified person will walk in off the street and ask for a job. This seldom happens.

The volunteer system does have its strengths: those who volunteer for service are usually quite dedicated and generous. But dedication and generosity carry no guarantee of competence and vision. How many volunteers have worked hard to get on boards of education in order to "force them to start using the Baltimore Catechism and begin teaching real religion again"?

Leadership Training

An alternative approach to the volunteer system is to identify those who have a willingness to serve and a potential for leadership, and then recruit and train them. This may mean motivating them to serve because they may not possess the motivation of volunteers. But this approach allows pastoral leaders to have the initiative on their side, seeking out those who could make a real contribution to the parish if they were properly motivated and trained.

How did Jesus establish the Church? Not by waiting for people to seek him out; he went into the streets and along the waterfront recruiting. He chose men for service and asked them to follow him. He chose some very unlikely people: fishermen are not generally at the forefront of religious revolutions. But he saw in these men he chose the potential for them to become the foundation of his Church. He walked up to them when they were busy with their nets and accounting books and asked them to set those things aside so that they could serve him. And they did this.

Jesus did not leave matters there. If he had, he would have had fishermen leading his Church instead of apostles. Instead, Jesus spent much time in training his disciples: he took them aside and taught them about service to the kingdom, and then sent them out on practice missions. Their basic training consisted of watching Jesus himself do the works that they would later undertake.

If a pastor were to adopt a similar program today, he would look around him for men and women who possess the potential to be of service to the parish. He would be sensitive to the broad variety of gifts that exists among his parishioners, and to the many different kinds of service that need doing. He would conceive of himself as a "talent scout," and try to match up those with latent skills to the various identified needs in his parish.

If his parishioners required motivation or training, he would undertake this challenge. It is a challenge, incidentally, that can be met: the Cursillo as it was developed in Spain was precisely a means of motivation and training for men with the potential for Christian leadership—even if they were not "church goers" before they went on the Cursillo.

Vision and Discernment

Of course, this presupposes that the pastor possesses a vision of what should be happening in his parish, and knows his parishioners well enough to discern their individual talents. It also presupposes that the pastor will not feel threatened by lay men and women undertaking tasks that have been tacitly left to the clergy in the past. Who says it must be a priest who handles pre-marriage interviews and instructions? Why couldn't a mature married couple handle it? And perhaps more effectively. This approach also presupposes that the pastor is willing to make a big investment of himself in training those he recruits—for it will be his generosity in giving of himself that will call forth generosity from others. The example of Jesus must always stand as the model for training lay leaders today.

Aggressive recruiting and training of lay leaders will not completely solve the problem of dwindling clergy: the Church is essentially sacramental, and a priestly presence is necessary in every parish. But it is an active, rather than passive, approach to meeting the problem. It is an attempt so thoroughly to integrate the members of a parish into its mission that the loss of an assistant, or even a resident pastor, would not be a devastating blow. It is an approach that models itself on Jesus' way of staffing the leadership and service positions in his Church.

Perhaps pastors should imagine that they will remain only three more years in their parish as pastor—and that there will be no replacement for them when they leave. If they acted on this assumption, their path would be clearly defined. They would place the highest priority on selecting, motivating and training lay leaders who would carry on as much as possible the mission of the parish after the pastors themselves were gone. The results of three sustained years of such an approach should be quite significant. Even revolutionary.

Leon McKenzie

The Art of Delegation

Two corporals were vying for promotion to the rank of sergeant. The captain decided to settle the issue by posing a problem for them to solve. "How would you get a flagpole painted?" the captain asked. Corporal Smith stated that he would requisition some paint, paint brushes, and an extension ladder, and that he would begin painting at the top of the pole and gradually move the extension ladder to lower heights. The captain looked at Corporal Jones for an answer. "The problem is quite simple," said Jones. "I'd tell two privates to paint the pole." Jones was promoted, as he should have been; he was a born leader.

The delegation of work is one of the most important themes in managerial studies, and I wish to approach the concept of delegation in terms of the management of a parish or local church. The word "manager" is used to designate the pastor, the parish council, or anyone in the parish responsible for completing tasks and reaching goals.

Four Orientations Toward Delegation

There are four basic stances taken by managers who confront delegation. These orientations range from a total rejection of the use of the process to a maximum reliance on delegation strategies.

1. *"I'll do it myself."*

Many managers are tempted to disregard delegation completely. These managers assume that the only way to get a job done is to do it themselves. At first glance, this attitude toward delegation seems to be supported by a random selection of our past experiences. When people do something themselves the job gets done the *way* it should be done, and, usually, *when* it should be done. But there are deficits to consider about this feeling toward delegation.

When a manager does everything, the law of diminishing returns soon takes its toll. One person is capable of performing only so much work and decision-making. Managers who insist on doing everything themselves eventually overload their circuits and find that they can do few things really well.

Other deficits in this approach toward delegation must be noted. The non-delegating manager does not involve others in the management of the parish. This lack of personal involvement leads inevitably to an increasing lack of interest within the parish community. When people invest themselves in the work and decision-making that affect the parish, they are more likely to manifest a high degree of commitment to the parish as an organization.

Non-delegating managers also implicitly "tell" others that they do not trust their abilities—a subtle but sure way of creating conditions to alienate people from the parish organization.

2. *"You do it this way."*
Some managers delegate tasks but plan precisely in advance how the task will be done. This kind of manager retains a great degree of control over the functioning of the delegate. Usually a greater quantity of work gets done, but what are the disadvantages to this approach?

When delegates are not permitted to plan—when they are not allowed to engage in decision-making—they are reduced to the status of a menial. They become mechanical men and women. They feel that the manager has truly little confidence in their rational abilities. The degree of their involvement—and the degree of their personal self-investment in the task—is marginal or low. They sense that their muscles are being put to work but not their minds, and their spirit.

3. *"You do it your way and I'll watch."*
Some managers delegate both physical tasks and the authority to make decisions. This is true delegation. In the first two orientations toward delegation we were really talking about assigning work to others. Most definitions of delegation in the literature of organizational behavior stipulate that delegates should have decision-making responsibilities.

When the manager says, "I'll watch" he is merely reserving the option of operational oversight or the option of *concurrent monitoring*. There is nothing wrong with this. Most delegates realize that the buck stops passing with the manager and do not resent being monitored.

This approach to delegation and to getting things done is more effective than the two approaches considered previously. Delegates are allowed to become involved in the work; they are permitted to make decisions; they are generally more committed to the task because they experience a degree of self-investment in the work—the investment of their minds as well as their bodies. They feel trusted.

4. "You do it your way and then tell me about it."

The final orientation toward delegation is the most "open." The manager makes maximum use of the talents of the delegates. The manager evaluates the work and decision-making after the fact; he relies on *retro*spective monitoring. In most situations this approach is very effective and very productive, not only in terms of getting things done but also in terms of providing for the personal satisfaction of the delegates. A word of caution: retrospective monitoring should not be used when the task that has been delegated is extremely complicated or will have far-ranging negative consequences if it is not done well.

The Art of Delegation

Delegation is not a strict science that follows unchangeable natural laws. The manager's selection of an orientation toward delegation depends on a thorough analysis of each specific situation. The manager's artful "reading" of each different situation will dictate which of the four stances toward delegation is most appropriate.

The art of delegation also involves explaining to others why a particular stance was taken by the manager. Again the art of delegation concerns the attempt on the part of the manager to be as consistent as possible through the selection of a *prevailing* orientation. To select four different orientations on four different days—with no apparent justification—only causes frustration and confusion in potential delegates.

A number of other variables come into play when the manager selects an orientation toward delegation for a particular case: the manager's personality and the personalities of the potential delegates, the manager's realistic appraisal of the abilities of potential delegates, the relative importance of the work and decision making, and the amount of time available for task completion. It must be stressed again, there is no scientific formula for the selection of an orientation toward delegation. Managers must become as artful in their way as Machiavelli was in his, but benevolently.

Delegation and Managerial Character

To delegate and obtain the most benefits from delegation the manager must possess a unique character composed of three qualities: trust, patience, and humility.

The delegating manager must be trustful of the abilities of others to get things done. Lacking the quality of trust, the manager will delegate responsibilities and then continue to meddle in the work of the delegate. The consequences of this type of behavior are obviously destructive. The manager who is constitutionally unable to trust delegates should not even think of delegating work and responsibilities to others. He is not equipped to be a true manager.

Delegating managers must be patient. When managers delegate work and responsibility they must be able to tolerate apparent bumbling and unmet deadlines. Lacking patience, managers will become anxious and communicate this anxiety to the delegates. This merely makes the work of the delegates more difficult, and often impossible.

Finally, delegating managers must be humble. Those in managerial positions think that their ways are obviously the best ways and that delegates could not possibly do a better job than the managers. This tendency toward arrogance and self-illusion is present in all of us, in varying degrees. Managerial humility should be the kind of humility identified by Thomas Aquinas: the clear-sighted view of the truth. And the truth is that all of us are limited, fallible, and restricted in our knowledge and competence simply because we are human. The truth is that many of the people who are "followers" are much more knowledgeable and competent than those who have achieved a position of leadership.

"Know thyself!" urged Socrates. Managers who possess an accurate knowledge of *self* will always admit their shortcomings and foibles. Strong managers alone feel comfortable about admitting their weaknesses and limitations; weak managers are too uncomfortable with their weaknesses to admit them. When strong managers admit their limitations, they recruit others to help them get the job done. When managers deny their limitations, they plod along by themselves, and eventually fall victim to the immutable law of diminishing returns.

Conclusion

Since I began with an anecdote with a military setting, it seems appropriate to conclude with a reflection on the words of General George S. Patton: "Don't tell a man how to do a thing. Tell him what you want done, and he'll surprise you by his ingenuity."

What lies at the heart of Patton's observation is the assumption that there is a creative spark in most human beings: given half a chance, people will respond to challenges with enthusiasm and resourcefulness. In delegating responsibility, managers let people know that they recognize their creativity, competence, and resourcefulness. And the bottom line is this: *more* work gets done, higher *quality* work is done, and the human relations climate improves immeasurably which, after all, is the goal of every true manager.

Part III

The Parish Council

At the heart of parish change is the parish council. At one moment the council seems to be no more than a rubber stamp for the pastor. At another moment it appears to usurp the pastor's legitimate power. In one parish the council attends only to financial matters; in another it turns its attention to the whole gamut of parish problems.

Bishop Frank J. Rodimer outlines the role of the parish council in the first article in this section. Bishop Rodimer is the ordinary of the Diocese of Patterson, New Jersey, and a long-time advocate of parish councils.

James R. Trent, another long-time proponent of parish councils, writes about shared decision-making in the second chapter in this section. His reflections are integral to the new styles of leadership in today's Church.

Patty Coleman contributes the third chapter, a psychological interpretation of much of the failure councils experience. Ms. Coleman is a popular freelance writer and speaker.

Frank J. Rodimer

The Work of the Parish Council

Back in the sixties when we began to hold dialogues with Protestant ministers, I remember once telling a clergyman from a church with a tradition for congregational administration of our plans to establish parish councils in all our Catholic communities. I told him of our new enlightenment and of our need to get everybody involved in decision-making. When I finished I waited for his approval. The wait was a little longer than I had expected, and he finally remarked, only half kidding: "You Catholics must be out of your minds! You should have checked with us before you got going into this."

There have been times in the past decade when I believed he was right. We've all made our share of mistakes, and we're still making them—hopefully new ones, not just the same ones all over again. In some ways, we're still off track. We've been frustrated, angered, disillusioned. Some have given up. One pastor recently told me—and I believe him—that when he went to his new assignment, responsible people begged him not to resurrect the council that had folded in bitterness under the previous pastor.

We've had our share of successes, too. A lot of favorable changes have taken place, a lot of movements have flourished, many of our worthwhile institutions still thrive, and these things have happened everywhere in the Church. The honest efforts made in parishes by priests, religious and laity to consult, consent and collaborate have meant that the Church on the parish level is, for the most part, alive and well.

That we've had frustrations—heartburn, headaches, insomnia and emotional outbursts that have sent us to the

Reconciliation Room—shouldn't be too great a shock. If ever a whole people were green and naive in an undertaking, it has been Catholics trying to form parish councils and to function with them. What did we have to go by? Some scriptural references to idealistic communities with no structural resemblance to our own. Some excellent theological statements in Vatican II on decentralization and shared responsibility, a few expert treatises on authority and a host of sophomoric interpretations of them by greenhorns.

Vatican II said very little specific about parish councils except that they should exist. Beyond that, it offered a statement on the laity that is delightful as a classic demonstration of naivete: "The laity should develop the habit of working in the parish in close union with their priests, [a footnote tells us that Pope Leo XIII said this in 1894], (and) of bringing before the ecclesial community their own problems, world issues, and questions regarding man's salvation, to examine them together and solve them by general discussion" (Vatican Council II: The Conciliar and Post Conciliar Documents ed. A. Flannery, O.P., "Decree on the Apostolate of Lay People," par. 26, pp. 791-792). The miracle, when you think of it, is that with so little to go on, we've come as far as we have.

One other reason for all the frustrations is that many people expected too much too soon. They expected instant success with a change in structure. Someone said Pope John called on the Church to open its windows and let in some fresh air; we opened them, and in came a lot of strange birds.

But we've also expected too much of one another. Priests expected the laity to understand their problems, to pick up the mantle of responsibility, to do more than talk, and certainly to do more than grab the checkbook. People expected their priests to understand all their problems, to turn over everything to them, to do nothing without consultation and approval. All wanted the new structure to bring everybody—liberal and conservative, old and young, men and women, married and single, white collar and blue collar, laity, religious and clergy—into unity and harmony, into instant community. It was a goal impossible and unreal.

Henri Nouwen put it this way: "No friend or lover, no husband or wife, no community or commune will be able to put to rest our deepest cravings for unity and wholeness. And by burdening others with these divine expectations, of which we ourselves are often only partially aware, we inhibit the expression of free friendship and love and evoke instead feelings of inadequacy and weakness."

Amen. That's precisely what we've done—burdened others with "divine expectations." We wanted parish councils to heal all wounds of division, to solve all problems. We were as gullible as people I remember as a child who listened to the medicine man make his pitch on the back of his truck and then bought his elixir for one dollar a bottle to cure everything from falling hair to athlete's feet.

We've done and said what we've thought was right and then we expected everybody to understand and accept it. Being human they didn't. Sometimes, we reacted, inhibited their freedom and scared them off. Or they did the same to us.

The parish council as a new structure is not what creates community; it is not what makes us one. The Spirit of God, the Holy Spirit, the Love of Christ, that is what unites us.

If we have been expecting too much of one another personally, we also must ask whether our parish councils are dealing with the right subjects to begin with. What do parish councils accomplish? Here are the latest statistics for our diocese: As of today, 28 of our 102 parishes have submitted their pastoral reports for last year. Of these, 21 have parish councils— that's three out of four.

Under the question: "What major issues did the council deal with last year?," various answers were given, and I've put them under categories—some parishes, of course, listed more than one accomplishment:

Finances—12
Property-maintenance—11
Social life-calendar—4
Catholic school issues—3
Religious education program—3
Liturgy—3

(one parish dealt with special ministers of the Eucharist;
another with a folk Mass; another with the problem of
finding a meaningful liturgy for youth.)
Community or social programs—2
(one instituted a Big Brother program)
Census—1
Return of those who left Church—1
Spiritual renewal—1
Communications (newsletter)—1

The parish council should deal with finances, prepare and
approve and check on the budget. It should be concerned
about the properties and the social calendar. But this is all
housekeeping—important, essential, but introspective and
only indirectly apostolic. What is the purpose of the
parish—survival? All right, budgets, maintenance and calen-
dars are all that's needed. But that isn't the purpose of the
Catholic parish. The parish is a community of people who
believe in Jesus Christ as their Lord, Saviour and guide, who
listen to the word of God and strive to live its message of
love, who worship together and receive their strength from
the Eucharist they share, who seek their own sanctification
and that of the whole community. That is the mission of a
parish. That is the ministry of the parish council.

Think about that: parish council members are ministers.
We've come to realize more clearly in recent years that a person doesn't have to be ordained to be a minister. Baptism and
Confirmation give us the basic character and identification
with Christ to proclaim the Word of God as lectors; also to
distribute the Eucharist in Mass and to the sick. Yes, and to
minister to the community as parish council members by
coming up with plans of action and by implementing them to
reach many segments of society: disenchanted youth, the
abandoned poor, the neglected elderly, those who have
drifted away, and all the faithful who expect, or who may not
even know they need, a better liturgy, or who should have
greater opportunities to be educated in their faith. I've heard
someone say that the ministry of the parish council is just
beneath the role of the deacon in the community. I'd say
that's about right.

We know enough about what we've done right, and what we've done wrong, to be able to say what we need to do in the future.

The first thing a council must do is to pray. The parish council is not a board of directors, not a blue-ribbon panel, not a house of representatives—though, hopefully, it does represent a broad cross section of the parish. Council members are a group of people trying with the grace of God to discern the voice of the Holy Spirit, trying to be one with Christ, trying to acknowledge his presence in their midst.

Membership on the parish council requires a greater effort towards personal sanctity and towards patience and humility. We must listen and fight not with others, but with ourselves, with our inclination to react to whatever is said.

I recall with horror how years ago a college student came before our parish council and made a long idealistic speech about the Church. When he was finished, he was shot down as one member refuted him point by point. The young man didn't respond further; he left and never came back again. This tragedy is repeated constantly in our parishes, and we still ask: Where are our youth?

It takes humility, patience and personal sanctity to listen to God and to those through whom He speaks. A council member should be a holy member of the community, i.e., a person working towards holiness. It should not be necessary to say that if the member is a Catholic that person should be a strong practicing Catholic, a recognizable Christian.

Not only personally, but as a body, the council must pray. Every meeting should include scripture reading, some study program, spiritual exercise, and at least once a year, the council should have a day of Recollection, and if possible, a weekend retreat. The best thing our parish council ever did was to experience a full 40-hour-in-one-week retreat given by the Better World Movement.

Recently the Diocese of Paterson dedicated "Bethlehem-in-Chester," an effort led by Fr. Eugene Romano to provide the desert experience to counteract the lemming-like instinct in us Americans—rushing towards self-destruction. We need quiet, contemplation, prayer—otherwise our efforts to create a Christian community are doomed to failure.

The second need of a parish is conversion to a sense of community, to an understanding of the parish as a community. We start with the pastor. Fr. Lombardi, S.J., founder of the Better World Movement, gave a retreat to bishops during Vatican II, and dealing with the parish he gave the bishops a plan of action. "The first essential step," he said, "is a profound conversion of the priests to a sense of community. This is your delicate, difficult responsibility. You must make sure that the priest in charge of souls becomes convinced that he is responsible not only for the spiritual welfare of a given number of individual souls but for creating among the members of his parish a genuine fraternal spirit."

That conversion of priests is not a foregone conclusion, and this fact need not shock anyone. The understanding of the Church—and of the parish—as a community is not dominant in most people's minds. The parish as an institution is. That's why most parish councils consider their main area of activities to be finances, properties and schedules.

Fr. Avery Dulles in his fine book, *Models of the Church* (Doubleday, Garden City, N.Y.), gave five concepts of the Church:

1) Institution—which stresses organizations and concentrates on buildings, rules, regulations, roles of pope, bishop, pastor, priests. (I saw a cartoon recently, with the parish council president explaining the meaning of the Church with her hands forming the old, familiar: "Here's the Church, and here's the steeple . . . .") That's what the institution model tends to do: "Here's the pope, here's the bishop, here's the priest, here are the people."

2) Community—which stresses parish as family or community bound by ties of faith, grace, love. This model is characterized by such terms as Body of Christ, People of God.

3) Sacrament—which stresses parish as a sign of Christ's presence in our midst. Parish is the place where Christ's love appears most clearly and reconciles men to God and to one another.

4) Herald—which stresses parish as a place where the word of God is preached and taught, and faith is professed.

5) Servant—which stresses parish as people who heal,

help, and serve people in need, a parish with strong social action programs.

A parish should include the best elements of all five models but if one is to be primary it should not be the Church as institution. And if, to all or most involved, it is, conversion is needed.

The third need of a parish council is for growth, maturity, the need to change, to accept the importance of change. "To live is to change, and to be perfect is to change often." So said John Henry Newman.

I once knew a man who had strong progressive plans, and he told me: "We'll have to work hard to put things in order, but once we do we can sit back and relax." Perhaps I misunderstood him, but taken at face value his words and sentiment were dead wrong. We'll never get to a point where our work is done, and we'll never get everything reformed once and for all. Because of our humanity the Church is always in need of reform.

The historian, David O'Brien, said that the Church is always in a crisis because it does not have control over the culture and society around it. It is always in the position of responding to forces beyond its control. The basis of our response always must be the love God shares with us and the truth He has revealed to us through Christ and the inspiration He gives us as Church.

Rudd Bunnick wrote, "It is certain that tomorrow's ministry, however much it continues that of today, must be different, otherwise it would no longer be a living ministry. The risk of a possibly inaccurate grasp is less (serious) than the risk of immobilism and ossification" (*Priests for Tomorrow,* Holt Rinehart and Winston, N.Y.).

Whatever changes that are needed for growth must be made. It's not a matter of one person's opinion; nor is it something determined by surveys. It's a matter of inspiration: What is right? The general catechesis follows.

The fourth need is for planning. Fr. Gustave Weigel, S.J., in a discussion said: "If you just let everything go, and take care of itself, it will all turn out in the end—badly!"

Each parish must have a statement of its mission. Why is it

there? What do the people agree to as its purpose? Not, what does the pastor or the Code of Canon Law say or anybody from the top of the mountain. When Moses was dialoging with Yahweh, the Israelites were down below carousing around a golden calf. The people are often on a level different from that of their priests; all must work to define the meaning of the Church and come up with a correct understanding of it.

What is the parish's vision? Where is it going? Are the paving and the roof the most important things a royal priesthood, a chosen people have to talk about?

What, then, are the major concerns of the parish? What are the goals under each of these concerns? What are the objectives for this year under each goal? Planning is absolutely essential.

Unfortunately, most parishes don't do much if any planning. Probably don't know where to start. That's why a growing number of dioceses have a Planning Office.

Under this category, I place the need for rudimentary training in the behavioral sciences. People are elected or appointed to parish councils and walk into a meeting cold, like Daniel in the lions' den. The parish council is sometimes the modern version of the early Christian gladiator combat.

Instead of interaction we often have reaction, and it takes a good president to know the difference, to detect it and to keep it from causing damage. Planning includes some training and education in interpersonal relationships. Good will is not enough. It has been responsible for some of the worst human destruction in history.

By now, we're experienced enough with our parish councils that we cannot be called greenhorns, but we're still young at this business of sharing responsibility. We're still learning. Perhaps we haven't done a lot of apostolic things, but we've done some few. We've fought like a family, but we've laughed together and we've exchanged the sign of peace.

We've kept our buildings, but we've placed greater emphasis on the altar and the Lord. We know we're human, but we know we are the People of God, the family of Jesus Christ, enlivened by the Holy Spirit. That's why we believe in parish councils. God's people are challenged to bring His kingdom to pass. The family of Jesus is challenged to make known his freedom and peace. The Holy Spirit moves us to pray and work and be together. It's not our idea, and we're not doing it just because we're told we must.

The parish council is the right way to conduct a Christian community. The right way is not always the easy way. Strident and cacophonous sounds have risen from parish halls these past 10 years. Each of us has said many noble things about the Church during this period, but: "If I speak in the tongues of men and of angels, but have not love, I am a noisy gong or a clanging cymbal" (I Corinthians 13:1).

What we believe, and what we must strive harder to show in our lives, is that if we understand ourselves to be a community of brothers and sisters who love one another we shall make beautiful sounds of praise to the Lord. After all, He, not we, started the whole thing.

James F. Trent

Shared Decision Making

Decision by consensus is not a technique but a product.
Decision by consensus is not a skill to be learned but the result of development of a relationship of trust.

Prior to Vatican II, decision-making at all levels of the Roman Catholic Church was primarily by authoritarian rule. This method was highly efficient, and, given the nature of our institutional structure, fairly highly effective. A power structure existed wherein it was very clear that the priest, the pastor, or the bishop was the one who had the authority to make the decisions. Others, either laity or cleric, given the situation, could be asked to serve as advisors or consultors. These could generate ideas and hold free discussion, but at any time the cleric in charge could say that, having heard the discussion, he had decided to do such and so. The efficiency of this method is obvious. The effectiveness also would seem to be available at the cleric's disposal. Notice I said "seem." The greatest temporal resource of the Church is our people. The effectiveness of a decision depended upon the involvement of the people in the *decision-implementation.*

Ordinarily we would say that it is difficult to get people to carry out a decision that they had no part in making. And this is true. But we are talking about pre-Vatican II, a time in which "Father knows best" was an ingrained concept, at least here in the United States.

And so the real effectiveness of the system depended upon whether the cleric was a sufficiently good listener to cull the right information on which to base his decision. The implementation, with some natural limitations, followed from respect to the position or even the personality of the cleric decision-maker. This was true unless the decision was about something the people didn't like, such as integrating schools,

interparish sharing, or other thorny matters. Then the decision effectively "plopped"; the other members of the Church
simply made a common decision not to support it.

The effectiveness of the method had other limitations.
Sometimes the actions taken were quite out of line with what
the decision-maker wanted. This was often the case where
communication was poor and the people misunderstood the
decision or disagreed with it. They were neither able nor sufficiently motivated to carry it out effectively.

This was the decision-making process of our not-so-distant
past, efficient and effective, given the structure and the mind-
set. Under it, we grew and developed, as children grow and
develop under caring and loving parents.

"But when I have become an adult . . . "

Vatican II proposed a maturity of Church in which all
members were seen as peers, brothers and sisters rather than
parents and children. It acknowledged role differences within
separate membership groups of the Church, but at the same
time stated that these differences were interdependent and
based upon the contribution of the gifts God gives through
one to the other. Leadership is a common gift, not owned by
any particular class or position. It is a gift mutually made by
all members towards proclamation of the Word, and the redemption of humanity.

The function of leadership is to serve. It is to involve the
whole Church in the liberating mission of Christ. To this end,
it is to serve by sharing valid information so that people know
what they are talking about, know what the topic signifies in
the life and the faith of those around the table, around the
parish, around the neighborhood, around the diocese,
around the city and beyond. It is to serve the sharing of information of facts and figures and also the hopes and dreams,
fears and anxieties which personally and collectively accom-
pany those facts and figures.

Leadership is to serve the making of free and informed
choices, choices based upon sufficient information so that all
possible alternatives and their consequences can be explored.

Leadership is to serve the making of effective committed
decisions because those who are to implement them know

what they are going to do. They know, too, why they are going to do it this way and what results to expect, what they want to happen as a result of their action or non-action.

Leadership of this sort can function only in an atmosphere of mutual openness, trust and acceptance. In this type of atmosphere consensus can be employed to reach those decisions important enough to warrant the effort.

Consensus is not the same as unanimity. Rather, it is a state of affairs where communications have been sufficiently open, and the group climate has been sufficiently supportive, to make everyone in the group feel that they had a fair chance to influence the decision. Someone then tests for the "sense of the meeting," carefully avoiding a formal procedure such as voting. If there is a clear alternative to which most members subscribe, and if those who oppose it feel they have had a chance to exert influence, then a consensus exists. Operationally it would be defined by the fact that those members who would not take the majority alternative, nevertheless understand it clearly and are prepared to support it. It is a psychological state which Edgar Shein has described well:

> "I understand what most of you would like to do. I personally would not do that, but I feel that you understand what my alternative would be. I have had sufficient opportunity to sway you to my point of view but clearly have not been able to do so. Therefore, I will gladly go along with what most of you wish to do."

This process demands time for all members to state their opposition fully enough so that they feel the others really do understand them. This is necessary so that they are not later obsessed by the idea that they could have made their point if others had only understood what they really had in mind. The function of leadership is to aid the listening process by clarifying, summarizing, paraphrasing and by sharing opinions and experiences.

The responsibility for this function does not reside in any one individual, including the pastor or chairperson. It is the responsibility of everyone who participates in the decision-making process. Leadership is the function of all, not the

few. The different aspects of this function may be handled
better by some instead of others, but all must recognize their
personal responsibilities within the process of gathering valid
information, making free and informed choices, and securing
committed decisions.

The process can be long, arduous and very often frustrat-
ing. Some will seek to short-circuit it by the easy expedient of
calling for a vote. The wiser heads will suggest a short break
for private prayer, personal reconciliation, and another cup
of coffee.

But why not vote? Because, frankly, contrary to popular
opinion and the American way of life, voting does not secure
agreement. And it does not guarantee commitment.

Voting demonstrates efficiency rather than effectiveness.
No matter whether it is under minority rule (few vote—most
abstain), simple majority (51 percent) or two-thirds or even
three-fourths majority, the fact remains that there will be
winners and losers. The losers most often will not actively
support the winners. The disappointed resistance may range
from indifferent non-participation to active opposition.
Losers will talk about what "they" (the winners) decided
rather than what "we" (the council, the parish) decided.

"Church," being both a mystery of God's action and a
diversity of human expression, cannot realize itself in competition, but rather in collaboration. The knowledge and the
ability of the whole working together is greater than the sum
of the contributions from individual parts of the whole. Decision by consensus is, outside of spontaneous and unanimous
consent, the most effective way of reaching greatness.

As I say this, I also say that conflict is a valuable asset, not
to be avoided or resolved but to be managed. Constructive
conflict with regard to ideas, approaches and solutions
should be viewed as helping rather than hindering the
consensus-seeking process. This constructive conflict is possible when members avoid arguing to attain victory as individuals but instead seek what is "right" according to the
collective judgment of the group.

The key to consensus is the feeling all members have that
they have stated their position as clearly as possible and that

this position has been both understood and weighed as the decision is made. If this happens, consensus is achieved, support given and the decision is embraced and owned. If this sense doesn't exist, ownership will not fully be proclaimed.

As a technique toward achieving this sense, a parish within our Archdiocese has developed a process of consensus value rating. It works like this:

When the topic under consideration has been developed to the point of decision, all information having been surfaced and evaluated, the chairperson asks each member to indicate his or her position on the topic. Each member may choose a number from 0 to 5. This number is, in effect, their last word on the topic. *O* means "Totally opposed to the topic." *1* means "Not in favor, but see some merit in it." *2* means "No, but I accept passage." *3* means "Yes, but I will accept non-passage." *4* means "Favorable, but with some reservation." *5* means "Totally favorable toward the topic."

The number-statements given by the members are added together and then divided by the total membership present. No abstentions are allowed. A total ranging from 4 to 5 (approximately 83 percent) is automatic passage. A total of 3 to 3.9 (43-83 percent) means an automatic tabling. A total of 0 to 2.9 (less than 43 percent) means an automatic rejection of the topic.

Granted that this process may seem mechanical and far from the ideal of full and total discussion leading to final consensus, it does carry with it a satisfaction and finality helpful to decision-making. Each has spoken and spoken effectively and positively. All statements have positive value, including *0* which must never be considered a veto, but rather a firm statement of differing opinion.

The Church of today calls for collegiality and a sharing of the gifts God gives to each of His people for the sake of all His people. One of the gifts given to the cleric is that of calling forth and coordinating the gifts of his brothers and sisters. Together they will decide the thrust and application of their gifts within their areas of responsibility.

In the final analysis, decision by consensus is a sign of neither efficiency nor effectiveness. It is a sign of trust, of understanding, of faith, and of acceptance.

It is a sign of a people, not in competition, but in cohesion. And such signs are most welcome.

Patty Coleman

Why Parish Councils Fail

Mary, Jack and Gertrude almost did me in. Perhaps you know them, or others like them. I hope not, but I fear that such people are found in many parishes. I met them not long ago when I was an observer at a parish council meeting. The meeting was a disaster. Not one single decision was made all evening. By the end of the session everyone in the room, myself included, was terribly depressed. As we said the Lord's Prayer together, I thought, "Indeed, Lord, deliver us from this kind of evil. Please send your Church a little hope."

This is how the sad story began.

Tom, a member of the finance committee, announced that he believed the janitor's salary should be raised. His proposal was clear-cut, his reasons convincing. He noted the need to keep pace with inflation, the injustice of the present salary and his fear that the janitor would quit if he didn't get a raise.

I was prepared to see the People of God go into action.

What I saw was three councillors turn the meeting into an unrelieved fiasco. And they did it in the name of piety and righteousness.

Mary was first. She had an all-too-familiar whining voice, one that seemed to cry out for the accompaniment of a funeral dirge. "Well, I don't know about a big decision like this," she began plaintively. "After all, we are supposed to make sacrifices for the Church. The janitor could get on with what he has. We've tried to raise salaries before and the people didn't like it at all. There's going to be a lot of opposition. Many of my friends make less than the janitor, you know."

As she droned on, Mary never lifted her eyes from the table before her. She seemed extremely sad. Only when she spoke of making sacrifices did she show the slightest animation. As I watched and listened with growing despair, she ran down. I

66

noticed that then she settled in for the rest of the meeting and
never uttered another word.

And yet, she did not have to say much more. There was sad
eloquence in the cast of her body, sacrificial, beaten. My own
self-confidence waned as I watched her. I think the other
members of the council, too, were afflicted by her contagious
melancholy.

Act II of the grim little tragedy opened as Jack, the local
liberal-in-residence, launched a long, impassioned oration on
the problems of the poor in the Third World, and social
justice. He progressed, somehow, to the teachings of the
popes from Leo XIII to Paul VI and in the middle of his talk
I forgot all about the janitor. After all, he doesn't live in the
Third World and the popes never knew him.

Jack's talk did help briefly dissipate the clouds of Mary's
residual melancholy but I soon noticed that he, too, was making me feel guilty and helpless. I didn't want the Third World
poor to be hungry. I didn't want to be caught in a web of social injustice and I surely didn't want to be at odds with the
popes.

Still, when Jack was through I was tired. Everything
seemed so hopeless and the world so desperately evil. "Good
grief," I thought, "what's wrong with me? I came to this
meeting with a bit of bounce in my heart and now I am feeling melancholy and guilty."

Still reeling from the first two punches, I was easy fodder
as the final act unfolded on Gertrude's little presentation. I
suspect the others in the room shared my uneasiness and
mounting despair.

"I'm ready for a salary raise," Gertrude began and I
brightened. "But, I want to be sure we do it right. I have
looked over the budget and I noticed that we are $3.97 short
of enough money for the janitor's raise."

At this point, I almost blurted out, "Let me give the
$3.97."

One council member did rise and sincerely offered the
missing money. But, Gertrude quickly shushed him. She pa-
tiently explained that things could not be done that way. A
budget was a budget, she said, and must be followed correct-

ly. "Why have a budget if we can't be correct?" she intoned with an air of firm righteousness.

To make a long and almost unbearable story short, the poor janitor never got his raise. All the king's horses and all the king's men could never get that council working again.

That night I left the meeting feeling melancholy, guilty, and frustrated by the long, pointless wanderings of the finance committee. It seemed impossible to accomplish any good. I noticed that Mary, Jack and Gertrude seemed a little relieved and just a bit more at ease as they left the meeting. Why, I wondered? What had they accomplished?

Later that night, I had a long session with my resident analyst who also happens to be my husband.

We talked about psychologist Carl Jung's description of humans' ambivalent states—how we all wish to be both a victim and a hero. When one "ego-state" becomes dominant, people lose their ability to function effectively.

We talked at length about the "victim ego state" since it was the victims who troubled me at the meeting. Victims actually enjoy failure. It makes them feel that they are suffering for the sins of the world as well as for their own sins. They avoid success; success might destroy their melancholy reveries and their soft enjoyment of self-pity.

Three ways of avoiding success are: (1) to point out the possible negative consequences, (2) to generalize the problem so it can't be handled, and (3) to insist on perfection to the point that nothing can ever be accomplished.

At the parish council meeting I saw all three tactics in action. Mary pointed out the trouble a decision would likely bring; Jack generalized until we all felt guilty; Gertrude insisted on perfection. No wonder the meeting ended in failure. Unconsciously, all three wanted failure. They were afraid of crisp, unadulterated success, and unprepared to handle it.

Jung tells us that we all enjoy a little failure now and then. We enjoy just a little pain and welcome a bit of a putdown. So far so normal. But when we let our desire for failure and pain control our lives, we and all around us are in serious trouble.

While it may be true in some theological sense that it was

through suffering that Jesus redeemed the world, life is much more than suffering. Life is birds singing, children playing, adults smiling, and people taking charge of the world and making it do what God intended. The Church, like all institutions in this world of ours, needs more heroism, more enjoyment of success, even if these arrive in small measure.

Enjoy Success

Jesus himself was heroic. He did not hesitate to take great risks and he gambled his whole future on his Church. As a Church we need less caution, less fear, less desire to fail. We need the good old-fashioned, capitalistic enjoyment of getting the show on the road and watching our work bear fruit.

The next time I meet with that parish council (surely in the dim, distant future) I plan to carry with me three messages, all couched in direct language. I want to tell Mary to look on the bright side and get off her melancholy kick. I want to tell Jack to cut out his high-blown generalizing. We don't need any more guilt trips, Jack, and for the overly efficient Gertrude, I plan to tell her to forget about perfection and look to the big picture. Let's make a few little errors so we can get some good done.

Although I was deeply affected, my role was passive. I was just an observer at the meeting. Perhaps the most I can hope is that some council member will some day summon up the courage to confront Mary, Jack and Gertrude. But what will people say about such a confrontation? What principles are involved here? Maybe there is a more perfect way to do all this? Ah, there it is. There is a little bit of failure by desire in all of us!

What about you? Do you recognize Mary, Jack or Gertrude, perhaps in yourself?

What about your parish council? Are you succeeding less and enjoying it more?

Part IV

The Problems of Renewal

Renewal is not all sweetness and light. No form of human growth ever is. Our changing styles of leadership and changing expectations of what parish should be, have brought many practical problems. Four of them are discussed in this section.

Dolores Curran, noted columnist, speaker and author, discusses the expectations of women in the renewed parish. She finds many inconsistencies between what is preached and what is practiced.

Two Jesuit priests, Thomas J. Sweetser and James Ewens, tackle the problem of rectory living as an obstacle to parish renewal. Father Sweetser has long been active in the parish renewal programs of the National Association of Priests Councils.

How can a parish find all the talent it needs to meet the rising expectations of its people? Margot Hover, author of many books and articles on family life, presents a workable solution to this problem.

Finally, William V. Coleman whose article opened this anthology, speaks about the problems of the layperson who works for the Church. Male or female, Church workers deserve better treatment than they are currently receiving.

Dolores Curran

Women and Their Male Chauvinist Church

Whenever I hear someone say that Catholic women aren't interested in women's liberation, I shake my head. Maybe they aren't interested in working outside the home. Maybe they don't want to say Mass. Maybe they even relish mopping floors, but that doesn't mean Catholic laywomen aren't interested in Catholic women's liberation.

Ask a Catholic woman if she thinks it's fair that she's handed the responsibility for the survival of religion in the home while her husband's responsibility largely ends when he marries her.

Ask her how she feels about her parish council's and her pastor's willingness to hand her the CCD program, the parish bazaar, and the eternal coffee pot.

Ask her how she feels when she hears herself described as an occasion of sin.

Ask her thoughts on this bulletin notice: "Men, too, will enjoy this speaker because he has many profound ideas."

Ask her what she thinks when she reads that a prominent ex-convict is worthy of ordination while Mother Teresa and Dorothy Day aren't.

Ask her how she feels after hearing a panel of priests explain that if she did her job, young people would stay in the Church.

Ask her why she has no decision-making power in a Church that wouldn't exist if a laywoman hadn't made the first decision.

Ask her why Adam's fall was Eve's fault.

Ask her reaction to hearing that of 173 saints commemorated by name in the new Roman Missal, only 28 are women and only two are parents. (Ask her how she relates

73

that to the classic statement: "Parents are the most important nurturers of faith.")

Ask her how she feels at a parish council meeting when they decide to hire a woman because she costs less.

Ask her how she feels when she's blamed for lack of vocations.

Ask her whether she'd rather have a married or unmarried priest counsel her on marital difficulties.

Ask her how she feels when she's told how she should feel about the Equal Rights Amendment.

Ask her why she should be satisfied with housework when Jesus said, "Mary has chosen the better way."

Ask her why she's never read the phrase, *spokeswoman for the Church.*

Ask her, too, about that revealing pulpit phrase, "Even the laywoman (can serve, should read, is worthy of God's love)."

Ask her reaction to a discussion on the ordination of women when she suddenly realizes both sides are talking about nuns.

Ask her reaction to attending a parish course or diocesan meeting and finding that 90 percent of the participants are women.

Ask her reaction about having to explain to the kids why dad doesn't bother to go to parish meetings or Mass.

Ask her how she feels when she hears that Humanae Vitae begins with the greeting, "Sons and brothers."

Ask how she feels when her pubescent sons start mocking her religious behavior.

Ask her reaction to hearing motherhood and virginity eulogized in the same Mother's Day sermon.

Ask her feelings when she expresses some of these feelings and is asked, "What are your qualifications to question the Church?"

Finally, ask her why she and her laysisters keep on furnishing the bulk of parish power in spite of a stacked deck.

Then tell me again that Catholic women aren't interested in women's liberation. Ha!

Thomas P. Sweetser, S.J. and James Ewens, S.J.

Are Rectories Obsolete?

There are many ingredients used in concocting a successful team ministry in a parish. There must be a basic compatibility among the team members, an agreement on future directions and goals for the parish, a sharing of ideas and expectations, a common theological stance and time together for prayer, liturgy and mutual support.

But there is one important ingredient that is often overlooked, one that has an influence on how well the team functions in the parish. This is the life-style that the various team members choose for themselves before they gather to assume the tasks they carry out in the parish.

It can put extra pressure on a team, for instance, if some of the members live where they work and others come to work and then return home after their job is finished. This means that some staff members regularly get away from the demands of the work while others can only escape their responsibilities on occasion. Here is a fictitious example of what could happen in a typical parish team ministry.

Clarifying Pastoral Needs

The staff at St. Euphoria's made the decision last year to work as a team. They made a retreat together and worked out the details of how the decisions of the staff would be reached by consensus. They clarified the work-loads of each person, realizing that all share the responsibility of ministering to the people of the parish. There was to be a pastor, but in name only. The entire team would share the ministry equally, no privileged positions, no hierarchy of command. They then requested and received permission from the bishop to function in this manner, and spent a number of months explaining the new concept to the parishioners.

The team members made an initial commitment to the parish and to one another that they would stay with the team for at least three years. They agreed to spend time together in prayer and sharing each week and to spend a few days together every six months for evaluation, goal-setting and renewal of their dream. But the team was in operation only six months when it became clear that one factor they had not considered was causing tension in the group, the fact that some of the team members lived over the parish offices and the others lived some distance away.

The team consisted of six members. (St. Euphoria's school closed three years ago and this provided resources for a larger staff.) There were two priests who lived on the second floor of the rectory. The first floor of the rectory held the parish offices and the basement contained a large meeting room for parish functions. There was one religious Sister who lived with four other Sisters in a convent attached to the neighboring parish, about two miles from St. Euphoria's. She took care of the elementary school religious education program. Of the three laypeople on the staff, one was single and lived a number of miles from the parish. Her job was directing the music and planning the liturgical program of the parish. The other two laypeople were a married couple who lived in the parish and were responsible for the adult and high school religious education program. They had two school-aged children of their own.

It soon became apparent that whenever a crisis or a need arose in the parish the priests were the first to be called. If a teacher needed a key, the scout troop needed a room, the senior citizens needed the coffeemaker, the response was always, "Call the rectory."

On the other end of the spectrum, the team members who lived outside the parish came for their regular work periods and meetings, but were not visible at parish functions such as dances and fund-raisers. The married couple had the responsibility of their children and the Sister her community. That left the priests to pick up the slack in the parish.

Finally, at one of their retreats together, one of the priests brought up the problem. He felt the pressure of always being "on call" while the others could remove themselves, once their tasks were completed, by physical distance. The other priest, the pastor, on the other hand, said he liked being available to the people at anytime of the day or night. This fit his understanding of ministry and priesthood. At that point the scheduled agenda for the day was dropped. The team spent the remaining time dealing with this "new" problem that they had not predicted would surface.

Points of View

These were some of the feelings and opinions that the team members expressed about their different life-styles:

The pastor: "I feel that my life is my work and the best place to carry on this work is in the rectory, close to the parishioners. When they need me, they can always reach me. They know right where to find me."

The other priest: "I, too, want to be available to the people. This is how I define my priesthood. But I also need regular time and space away from where the people can find me, a place just for myself. I'm afraid that if I don't cut down on the hours I work, I may not survive personally or professionally. But neither do I want to live alone. I need other people, fellow priests and friends, to support me in my priesthood."

The Sister: "I have a job to perform in the parish and I do my work here to the best of my ability. But I also have a life that is not part of the parish or of the team ministry. This part of my life is centered in my religious community of Sisters and with my friends. That's why I live apart from the parish. I do attend parish functions not related to my work in the parish, but only those I want to attend, not because I feel I must." (The single woman on the team said this was the way she felt as well.)

The married couple: "We really enjoy this work and are very happy to be part of this team ministry. We find the parishioners responding well to our programs. We would like to be able to put in more hours in the parish. But our children need us. And we need them. We need one another. The week-

end retreats and the extra evening meetings are starting to get
to us. But we are learning to cope with it and feel we will be
able to stick it out at least to the end of the commitment we
agreed upon.''

The team then drew up a list of pros and cons for living and
working in the same place. The list went as follows:

*Advantages of living
where you work*

*Drawbacks of living where
you work*

1. Availability is most important. Little things, if not
taken care of immediately,
can get to be big things. Better to settle them on the spot
when they happen.
2. Visibility never hurts. It's
important that people see
you regularly and know you
care for them. This is the personal touch.
3. Keeping in touch with the
situation. You know the feelings and expectations of the
people because you are with
them when they are hurting
and rejoicing.

1. Everyone needs privacy.
Distance is necessary for extra sleep, prayer, working on
personal projects, and recre-
ation.
2. Distance brings renewed
energy. Being away from the
scene brings you back with
fresh vigor and increased ob-
jectivity.
3. Living away brings new
experiences. Having contact
with others outside the con-
text of the parish brings new
ideas and experiences that
can help the parish.

The list was much longer of course, but these items covered
some of the most important ideas of the group. As the retreat
progressed, it became apparent that, perhaps, it was time for
experimentation.

Over the next few months the team would look for a house
to rent, located a few blocks from the present rectory. The
house would provide the priests' living quarters. The team
felt that moving the residence just a few blocks away from the
rectory would provide enough distance for the priests. This

separation would prevent their being called on for every detail of the parish but leave them close enough so that they would be on hand if a real emergency arose. The present living quarters in the rectory would be maintained for guests and for the members of the team if they wanted a place to stay overnight on special occasions. This was especially true of the Sister and laywoman who lived some distance from the parish.

The team went home feeling tired, but happy with their new plan. The pastor contacted the bishop and although reaction to the plan was not enthusiastic, the bishop did give them permission to try it out for one year, as an experiment.

The reaction from the people in the parish was more enthusiastic. Only a few felt they were being abandoned by their priests. The general reaction was congratulatory. Most were happy that the priests were finally getting out from under the pressures of the parish. They felt there might be even more contact between the priests and people since the rectory would no longer be the buffer between the priests and parishioners. The team was surprised at how well the people accepted the idea and how much of an "ivory tower" image the rectory had in the minds of the people. It was as though the people felt that they "owned" the parish more now since the priests would be living in the neighborhood like everyone else.

There is a risk that any parish team will be divided into two groups, those who spend all their time in parish work and those who have a job to perform in the parish but work a set number of hours each week. The risk is that this latter group becomes "second-class" in comparison to those whose life is their work. A change of address for the priests and other religious members might help overcome this unintended class structure in the parish team.

But the problem goes deeper. At issue is the life-style of priests and the close relationship that exists between their work and their personal lives. In the past this relationship was never called into question. It was taken for granted that the parish priests lived in the rectory of the parish they served. But then the number of vocations to the priesthood began to drop and with this came the prediction that there would be fewer parish priests. At the same time the concept of team ministry surfaced as one way of dealing with the shortage of priests to serve in parishes. With this new approach to parish ministry, however, came new alternatives to how parish ministry is related to the people's personal lives. The rectory or convent is no longer the only place where parish ministers live. Some live in small communities, in apartments or in homes where they raise families of their own. So, with these alternative life-styles for parish ministers, it is only natural that many priests begin to realize that the rectory may not be the only place for them to live.

Margot Hover

The Problem of Talent

What I propose is that parishes adopt a "Supermarket Approach" to hiring staff members for the services they want. Initially, of course, those responsible for hiring must be able to define what they want. Do they want someone who will take from their shoulders the responsibility of organizing the CCD program? Do they want a person who will be capable of offering classes to the parish adults in various aspects of theology, scripture, psychology, and other topics of interest to involved Catholics? Do they wish someone who will visit the sick and dying of the parish, possessing the ability to relate to them in a healing way? Are they looking for someone who will help to deal with hostility that may be smoldering? Or do they want someone who won't precipitate confrontation? Do they wish to begin a program for families? for single parents of the parish? for members who want to become involved in social issues?

Some of these functions can best be performed by parishioners. It is a waste of time and energy to hire someone with an advanced degree in a specialized area to coordinate the dispensing of juice and cookies to preschoolers. And how many parish feuds could be avoided if those who are affected by the scheduling of classes actually did the scheduling? It is a truism that people do not attend programs in which they have nothing invested. Why do parishes hire people to do those things that will increase involvement—and attendance—if the parishioners themselves actually do them?

Multiple Resources

As the involved Catholic's interests become more sophisticated, it is increasingly difficult to find one person with adequate knowledge in all of the areas that should be covered in a good parish education program. Outside resources are an absolute necessity, regardless of the staff's qualifications. There are agencies, both Church affiliated and secular, that can help a parish in the search. Again, contracting for specific services frees funds to finance this type of consultation.

Once the parish is in touch with its needs and priorities, it can begin to look for resources. If catechist training is a priority, many diocesan staffs are eager to provide speakers for workshops and lectures for very reasonable fees. Children learn the same way, regardless of their religious affiliation. Public school media specialists and psychologists, local craftspeople and Scout trainers, public library personnel, Sunday school methods and crafts instructors—all can contribute their expertise in the general areas of teaching techniques. Many religion text publishers are pleased to be asked to send their authors and area representatives to parishes to give workshops in the utilization of their materials. Increasingly, self-instructional materials are available in the form of tapes and workbooks. With a parishioner to coordinate the effort, groups of catechists could process this material together, sharing from one another's insights and experiences.

If adult education is a priority, the education committee must design a vehicle for determining the specific interests of parishioners. Once this information is gathered, it is relatively painless to locate resources to deal with those interests. Local educational institutions, clergy members with special training and skills, certified hospital chaplains, members of medical ethics committees, physicians, diocesan seminary faculty members, and other members of the local community have much to offer. Too often, talent in the parish is overlooked in the rush to find it elsewhere. Parish doctors, lawyers and counsellors, all have information and can provide insights into many of the issues confronting Catholics in the world today.

Professional religious educators are usually, at some step along the way, involved in liturgy. A creative teacher will be able to plan exciting liturgical experiences for classes, but more is needed if the liturgies are to be based in good theological and dramatic principles. National Catholic newspapers and catechetical journals list numerous publications that are specifically designed to help catechists plan good liturgies. On a broader scale, there are available aids which deal with the formation of effective parish liturgy committees and offer ways to prepare members to deal with various components of good liturgy. Publishers also offer workshops for parishes on various topics. This would be a good occasion to involve several parishes sharing locale or interest to pool financial resources for such a venture. Spending money in this manner has an added advantage: people tend to give more attention and credence to an "imported" speaker than they do to local staff members whose presence is familiar.

If parish leaders who are involved in the hiring of personnel to manage educational programs protest that they do not know enough about their needs to manage the program themselves, there are two responses. To hire a professional without knowing what you want is grossly unfair to the professional. Second, this is an abdication of responsibility. The furor over sex education in public or parochial school programs and the conflict in many parishes about the replacing of traditions surrounding First Communion lead one to the conclusion that parish leaders do, indeed, know what they want. Rather than play expensive guessing games with parish personnel, it would be by far the better choice to do the homework required to determine parish needs and priorities, and then to contract with individuals and agencies to provide the services that seem indicated.

The day of the empire-builder in parish religious education is—or should be—over. It is time for parishioners to take responsibility for the process of their parish life. This assumes that they take steps to educate themselves about the needs felt by members of the parish community; the resources resulting from this "Supermarket Approach" will probably be a far cry from the patterns with which we have grown comfortable. Who says that will necessarily be bad?

William V. Coleman

Working for the Church

This past spring a youthful DRE with seven years of highly successful experience told me he was leaving church work. He gave as his reasons, a low salary and no hope of future advancement. The parish in which he works has already witnessed the resignation of two young priests and three Sisters.

That same day a diocesan religious education director confided to me that he was hiring a 23-year-old woman to undertake the sensitive task of catechist formation. Her total experience was one year as a parish DRE.

Later in the week I learned that a youth minister I know will lose his job during the summer because his new pastor prefers a professional musician to a youth minister on his parish staff.

These stories make the rounds of those who work for the Church. Few gatherings of church workers are complete without complaints of poor working conditions, low pay and a lack of security. The morale of those who direct our church programs is not high. Such poor morale promises to undermine our best efforts at renewal.

Perhaps it is time to ask ourselves what makes a good job, in the Church or out of it. Let me mention five key ingredients:

1. Pay: Pay must be high enough to provide for a family and to allow that family to live in a social setting which demonstrates some achievement of success.

2. Status: A position should provide sufficient prestige to convince the workers and those around them of their worth and respectability.

3. Security: Employees need to know that what they are working to attain will not be taken from them by the whim of another, or by some unforeseen adversity.

4. Promotion: Employees must feel that if they work hard,

they can expect a higher echelon job with more responsibility, pay and superior status.

5. *Purpose:* Contented workers would like to be sure that their work contributes to a worthwhile goal.

Now, let's examine the situation of church workers against these criteria of a good job.

Pay is a problem. Many religious and laypersons are working for substandard wages. Religious workers often wonder whether they are hired because of their talent or because they can be paid a lower salary than laypeople. Increasingly, one hears them question their presence in upper middle class parishes where they seem to be saving money for those who least need financial assistance.

Status is not a problem if one is a priest or a religious worker. Laypeople, however, often have status problems. Many highly trained and competent laypeople find themselves working under an untrained and less competent clergyman. Why, they ask, is ordination a sign of competence while their own degrees and experience are not?

Security is a major difficulty for church workers. While priests and Sisters can expect life-long care from the Church, laypeople cannot. Many are forced to work without adequate hospitalization and retirement benefits. Few have any kind of tenure.

Promotion is almost non-existent in the Church. Few religious or laypeople can aspire to more responsible positions. These positions are often filled by those who have little or no experience but who are willing to work for substandard pay. Many church workers have reached the top of their profession before they are 30 years old.

Purpose is not a church problem. In fact, the sense of purpose among church workers is so great that many will accept sharp limitations in other benefits. It is the sense of purpose which makes church work attractive at all.

Today, our theologians speak learnedly of new ministries in the Church. They assure us that the clergy crisis is spawning new needs for lay and religious ministers. Here, they tell us, is the hope for tomorrow's church.

Perhaps the theologians are correct, but unless the Church

attends to the basics of good employment practices we may
well create new jobs and then discover we cannot attract the
talented people to fill them. Now is the time for a thorough
rethinking of what it means to work for the Church while
there are still enough enthusiastic and talented people who
want to fill our needs.

William V. Coleman

Problems of Renewal

Vatican II has brought and is still bringing a new spring-time to the Roman Catholic Church. Everywhere there are signs of new life and fresh vitality. According to the laws of sociology, this renewal should never have happened, and surely it should not have happened as rapidly and extensively as it has. Yet, the facts of Church renewal are present for all to see: a new liturgy with lay participation; new forms of diocesan and parish administration; a new idea of Church itself with its many ecumenical overtones; new techniques and content in religious education; and a whole new vision of parish life. These are among the most exciting years in the long history of Roman Catholicism.

The swift success of renewal has created new problems or perhaps exposed old problems, long ignored. Like the rapidly growing adolescent, today's Church is troubled by the size of its feet, its facial blemishes and the tight fit of its clothing. The inconveniences of growth are embarrassing and painful, but for the Church as for the adolescent they are the only sure signs of growth itself.

There is pain present in today's parish life. It is important to remember, however, that this pain is present only because of the success of the renewal. Today's problems are signs of yesterday's successes, and provide the challenge to prepare for a better tomorrow.

The single most important problem in parish life today is the recognition of women, and their increasing creative influence on parish growth. Fifteen years ago women had few roles of importance in the average local church. A woman might be the parish secretary in the relatively few parishes which hired secretaries. She might count the collection, answer the telephone and refer callers to one of the priests. If the pastor were very progressive, she might even be allowed to work on the parish bulletin, but always under his supervising eye.

If a woman was a religious worker, she might hope some day to be the principal of the parish school. As principal she looked to the pastor for guidance on all important matters ranging from finance to the discipline of unusual students. The pastor might even grant an unexpected holiday to the students without the knowledge or consent of the principal.

Women in the typical American parish of two decades ago played a consistently subservient role. There was little place for them in the public life of the Church, and little scope for their intelligence and creativity.

All this has changed. The change began in the mid-1960s with the recognition of the deplorable state of religious education in most parishes. Pastors began to attempt to solve the problem by hiring women to direct parish religious education programs. While many pastors then wished to think of the new DRE's as counterparts of the principal in the Catholic school, the forces of history were too great to allow this to happen.

The parish DRE soon discovered herself involved in more than the education of children. Parent education during the days of the liturgical changes was imperative. Many parishes looked to the DRE to undertake this sensitive work. Wider forms of adult education were soon delegated to the DRE. Sacramental preparation, youth ministry, liturgical education and planning and a myriad of other tasks were entrusted to the parish DRE. Few of the parish priests were willing or able to cope with these new demands.

By the mid-1970s the parish DRE was often the most significant parish minister and was charged with the most sensitive and demanding of the new ministries. In recognition of this fact, an increasing number of parishes have designated these women "pastoral assistants" or "pastoral associates." This change in terminology has given belated recognition to the fact that today's women are laboring side by side with men in the pastoral renewal of the Church.

In the first phases of this development religious women were more common than were lay women in parish ministry.

Studies indicate that today lay women are more numerous than their religious counterparts in the direction of religious education, if not in the unofficial pastoral ministry. There seem to be few distinctions drawn between lay and religious women in ministry. Their common goals and common experience have made them a solid, unified force in ministry.

Because of their rapid entry into parish ministry, women are now asking with some vigor why they may not also be ordained priests. They reason that they are doing all of the traditional work of the priest except to lead public worship. Why draw the line there and why draw the line on the basis of sex? They have proven themselves as competent as men, and as dedicated as men. When will high Church leaders accept the facts and permit ordination?

Church authorities have been reluctant to discuss this problem openly. While biblical scholars and leading theologians have offered no serious objections to ordination of women, the hierarchy has played a careful game. On one hand, they have denied that ordination of women can ever be possible; but on the other hand they continue to allow and even encourage women to take on more and more responsibility for ministry. Their whole response is difficult to interpret but they seem to be saying, "No for now, but let's see what can happen to make the transition to a female clergy easier."

A second problem which haunts today's local Church is the confusion over governance. There are no clear guidelines for the exercise of authority in the parish. In the Tridentine model of Church, all authority rested with the pastor. He was considered an almost absolute ruler within his parish and was held accountable only to his bishop. In practice, this accountability was limited to avoiding flagrant abuses of power and public scandal. As long as the pastor remained within the rather lenient bounds of clerical custom, he might do just about what he pleased within his parish. He was the parish equivalent of the medieval nobility.

Today this has changed. The reasons for this change have been three: the influx of a new type of staff, the growing independence of the laity and the advent of councils, boards and other bodies for parish direction.

Yesterday's staff consisted of priests trained to obey the pastor in all things while awaiting a pastorate of their own. With few exceptions, priests of the past did as they were told and could expect severe reprimands from the bishop if they failed to carry out his wishes.

Today's staff is very different. Priests who serve as associate pastors no longer see themselves as assistants to the pastor, but instead as semi-independent pastoral ministers. Religious women and lay men and women who work for the parish demand more independence and more responsibility than did the priests of the past. They can always resign if their demands are not met. Such resignations are the cause of severe pain in a parish and blemish the professional reputation of the pastor. The pastor who is not able to work with a staff is often reassigned to a smaller parish where there is no extensive staff to supervise.

Laity are more independent and are beginning to expect more of their pastor. As some parishes offer new and innovative programs, observant nearby parishioners will begin to lobby for such programs in their own parish. Once the support group of the pastor, today's educated lay people are often the most demanding part of his constituency.

Parish councils, parish school boards, commissions for religious education, liturgy and finance have all eroded the pastor's power. The parish has become so complex that no one person is any longer able to regulate all that is happening. At most, the pastor is able to give symbolic leadership and direction; he cannot govern the everyday direction of so many diverse programs. The parish councils, commissions, boards and committees often assume this role.

At the moment, few parishes know who has power over what phase of parish life. Staff, council and pastor all claim different sources of authority. One of the most pressing needs of parish life is clear definition of responsibility and authority. Next to the recognition of women, this is the most important current problem of parish life.

A third problem for today's parish is the growing tension between the clergy and the involved laity. The clerical system is unlike anything else in modern life. Modern life confers status on people for one of two reasons: educational attainment or professional competence. The only exception to this general rule is the status claimed by the small number of people with inherited money and power.

The clerical system, however, claims a high status role for all who have been ordained. Young men newly ordained are believed to be competent to undertake direction of any phase of parish life even though their educational attainments are modest and their proven competence next to none. Older men who have never proved their ability in some phases of parish ministry are expected to be able to direct these ministries solely *because* they are priests.

When priests were the only members of a parish staff and few people volunteered to accept serious responsibility in the parish, this system worked fairly well. Today, however, parish life is very different. Many lay and religious parish staff members are highly educated and have proven their competence beyond reasonable doubt. Many volunteers are themselves knowledgeable in theology and church life, and have spent years in attaining sensitive parish skills. Priests without knowledge and skills are often placed in supervisory positions over such people. The result is a debilitating tension for both the clergy and the other parish workers.

A crying need exists to establish true independence for professional and long-time volunteers in parish life and to remove them from clerical domination. Only in this way can the parish hope to avoid constant conflict and the loss of its most talented leaders. Vocations to the clerical state and to parish ministry will both be jeopardized unless this thorny problem is laid to rest.

Rectory living is yet another parish problem. An increasing number of priests feel that they should have a home of their own. They claim that the clerical-lay tension cannot be solved as long as the clergy live together in the parish rectory while the lay staff members have homes of their own. Further, they claim, it is unreasonable to expect men to live happily together only because they happen to be assigned to the same parish. They add that the minor irritants of common life have a way of becoming magnified when priests must work together closely all day long and then return to the rectory to spend their leisure time in isolation from the life lived by ordinary parishioners.

Religious women have experimented with solutions for this kind of problem for the past 10 years. Most religious communities now provide many different types of living accommodations for their members. They may live in the traditional convent attached to the parish school, live in an apartment with other Sisters or perhaps live in a convent attached to a school other than the one in which they teach. Such models may well be on the drawing boards for the parish priest.

Leadership problems in the parish certainly must include the present Church law on celibacy. Experts point out the growing shortage of clergy, the lack of seminarians, the age of today's clergy and the lack of vitality among those recently ordained. Other churches in the United States with members drawn from the same socio-economic background as Catholics are not experiencing similar clergy shortages. The only difference seems to be Catholic insistence on celibacy.

A change in this ancient Church law will bring great disruption to parish life in the opinion of many, but there seems little to be gained by continuing the present practice.

Not all leadership problems in the parish today center on the clergy. Lay people in parish ministry have special problems of their own. Recent arrivals to parish ministry, lay people have not yet achieved the working conditions essential to good professional development. These conditions are multiple: a reasonable salary, adequate freedom and responsibility, security and some reasonable hope for promotion.

Salaries for parish workers are continuing to escalate. Many parishes now pay their employees wages comparable to those of public school teachers. There seems to be a growing awareness on the part of parish administrators that only a reasonable salary will draw top talent to the parish. Adequate freedom and responsibility are increasingly being conferred on lay ministers. While the desired lay-clerical relationship is still far from established, many talented lay people have managed to find positions that do not include this problem because of the personalities and talents of individual clergy.

Security is still a major problem for parish workers. Few have contracts which extend for more than a few years. Many work without a contract or with contracts for just a single year. This kind of insecurity makes it difficult for the family person to devote high dedication to parish work. Too, many lay workers feel that although they work well with their present pastor a change of pastors would lead to reshaping the structure of the entire staff.

Hope for promotion is almost non-existent since individual parishes hire their own personnel and dioceses often hire the least experienced and least educated because of budget difficulties. The idea of promotion of lay people to positions of greater importance and responsibility is only now being considered by the most forward-looking Church administrators.

Most of the problems of parish leadership arise from the success of the many new forms of Church life. At the root of many of the problems is money. Catholics are not accustomed to supporting lay staff. As parishes increase their staff and involve more people in more programs, the need for parish support skyrockets. Certainly then, new patterns of church giving must be set unless the rapid development of leadership in today's parish is to flounder.

The success of the recent past has brought today's Church a series of painful problems. Many of these problems are being explored and solved piecemeal in the American Church. There is every hope that we as a body Catholic will respond to these problems in the years ahead and will find new problems that challenge our growing zeal.